Healthy Mindsets for
Super Kids

of related interest

Cool Connections with Cognitive Behavioural Therapy
Encouraging Self-Esteem, Resilience and Well-Being in Children and Young People Using CBT Approaches
Laurie Seiler
ISBN 978 1 84310 618 0
eISBN 978 1 84642 765 7

Helping Children to Build Self-Esteem
A Photocopiable Activities Book
2nd edition
Deborah M. Plummer
Illustrated by Alice Harper
ISBN 978 1 84310 488 9
eISBN 978 1 84642 609 4

How to Be Angry
An Assertive Anger Expression Group Guide for Kids and Teens
Signe Whitson
Foreword by Dr Nicholas Long
ISBN 978 1 84905 867 4
eISBN 978 0 85700 457 4

What Children Need to Be Happy, Confident and Successful
Step by Step Positive Psychology to Help Children Flourish
Jeni Hooper
ISBN 978 1 84905 239 9
eISBN 978 0 85700 483 3

Games and Activities for Exploring Feelings with Children
Giving Children the Confidence to Navigate Emotions and Friendships
Vanessa Rogers
ISBN 978 1 84905 222 1
eISBN 978 0 85700 459 8

No More Stinking Thinking
A Workbook for Teaching Children Positive Thinking
Joann Altiero
ISBN 978 1 84310 839 9
eISBN 978 1 84642 579 0

Starving the Anger Gremlin
A Cognitive Behavioural Therapy Workbook on Anger Management for Young People
Kate Collins-Donnelly
ISBN 978 1 84905 286 3
eISBN 978 0 85700 621 9

The Big Book of Therapeutic Activity Ideas for Children and Teens
Inspiring Arts-Based Activities and Character Education Curricula
Lindsey Joiner
ISBN 978 1 84905 865 0
eISBN 978 0 85700 447 5

Healthy Mindsets for
Super Kids

A Resilience Programme for Children Aged 7–14

Stephanie Azri

Foreword by Jennifer Cartmel

Illustrated by Sid Azri

Jessica Kingsley *Publishers*
London and Philadelphia

First published in 2013
by Jessica Kingsley Publishers
73 Collier Street
London N1 9BE, UK
and
400 Market Street, Suite 400
Philadelphia, PA 19106, USA

www.jkp.com

Copyright © Stephanie Azri 2013
Foreword copyright © Jennifer Cartmel 2013
Illustrations copyright © Sid Azri 2013

Printed digitally since 2015

Library of Congress Cataloging in Publication Data
A CIP catalog record for this book is available from the Library of Congress

British Library Cataloguing in Publication Data
A CIP catalogue record for this book is available from the British Library

ISBN 978 1 84905 315 0
eISBN 978 0 85700 698 1

To Julianna:
My forever kind and sweet daughter. You are the reason Healthy Mindsets for Super Kids *exists. I hope that it has been useful to you and I will always enjoy our memories of the programme together.*

To Killian:
My son... I hope that you had as much fun as I did participating in the programme. Remember 'WWW' always and KipKool!

To Sid:
Who would have thought we would publish a book as a family? Thank you for the hard work you've put into illustrating the Healthy Mindsets for Super Kids *programme. It wasn't easy but rejoice... It's finally over. Thank you.*

xxxxxxxxx

Love always, Mummy

Contents

FOREWORD

Those of us who confidently engage with our family members and the wider community sometimes take for granted the skills and attitudes required to function effectively as a member of these communities.

In taking the developing of these life skills for granted we overlook that some children in the middle childhood years do not have the benefit of confident family members to help them navigate their personal journey of growth and well-being. Further to that, children are increasingly spending more time outside of the family home during their waking hours. These are just two of the significant factors contributing to the emerging need for innovative responses to help children and the adults who support children to gain the life skills that build their resilience to cope with adverse circumstances in their lives.

Healthy Mindsets for Super Kids is an extremely useful resource for all those who support children in the middle years. Whether you are an educator in school-age care, a teacher, counsellor, youth worker or parent, the ideas contained in this book provide you with a systematic way to help children become more self-aware. Stephanie's style of writing and Sid's comic strips make this resource accessible to individuals working with children in a diverse range of settings. Stephanie anticipates some of the challenges implementing the activities; her hints and suggestions encourage facilitators of the sessions to reflect on their skills, review the ways in which they talk and listen to children and examine the role modelling they provide in all that they do – before, during, after and between sessions.

The resource was initially written and trialled in reaction to community need to support children with early symptoms of anxiety and depression. However, I commend this resource to all who work with children in the middle childhood years so that it is also used in a proactive way with all children to develop further their self-esteem, confidence and ability to manage positive and negative life events. The suggestions for the activities are meaningful to children and support their well-being, learning and development. The intent of the activities is to develop and extend children's life skills and to develop their dispositions towards citizenship, which in essence requires resilience and that includes a 'Healthy Mindset'.

Jennifer Cartmel
Senior Lecturer – Child and Family Studies
Griffith University, Queensland, Australia

Acknowledgements

I would like to acknowledge the people who made the *Healthy Mindsets for Super Kids* programme a success. First of all, my children for their needs, which sadly could not be filled in our local community forcing me to look at creative ways to fill the existing gaps. Second, to the organizations which agreed to trial the programme, without whose support it would not have had the chance to be evaluated like it did. Thank you to the Beenleigh Neighbourhood Centre for hosting the first intakes of the programme and Windaroo State School for hosting the programme since 2010. A particular warm 'thank you' to Ms Valerie Paterson, Deputy Principal, for her interest and faith in the programme and to Ms Angela Strong, the key woman who has been facilitating it, teaching many children resilience skills with compassion, care and vibrant energy at the school. Angela's enthusiasm has really been noticed and appreciated.

Thank you to Debbie Neale of ClickNColour (www.clickncolour.com) for providing us with the two art therapy samples (Grief and Loss Module 5). It is fantastic work, recommended to everyone. Of course, I would like to acknowledge Dr Jenny Cartmel for writing the Foreword of this book. Your expertise and kind words have been valued and embraced and I am forever grateful for having been mentored by you for the last few years of my PhD. I would be ungrateful if I didn't acknowledge Caroline Walton and her team at JKP for their ongoing and regular professional advice. Thank you.

But finally and foremost, thank you to all the families and children who have enrolled and participated in the programme since 2010. It has been fun and rewarding. Noticing your growth over the months has been a privilege. Please do not hesitate, ever, to let me know how the programme has made a difference in your or your children's lives.

BEHIND *HEALTHY MINDSETS* *FOR SUPER KIDS*

An Introduction

The notion of resilience emerged in the 21st century as an important factor influencing children's responses to adverse events, and in the last ten years, resilience theory and resilience programmes for children have flourished globally. While the concept started with the investigation of resilience of children of mentally ill parents, it continued with other at-risk groups such as children from low socio-economic backgrounds and those with learning difficulties (Werner 1993). It was quickly established that resilience was a theoretical shift towards strength-based models which would apply to all groups of children. In essence, resilience provides a framework for understanding theways and the reasons why children respond differently to difficult events. The definition of resilience has remained clear: resilience is one's ability to overcome negative events. However, it is believed that resilience is dependent on various factors such as personality traits, interactions with friends and family members, environments and access to resources and skills (Schoon 2006). Inherent in the concept of resilience is the principle that resilience should be regarded as positive and as an adaptation over time.

At an individual level, children's cognitive and psychosocial functioning affect their ability to overcome adverse events. Additionally, it is found that children's social skills, self-esteem, access to skills and resources, as well as a sense of belonging, foster resilience skills – the ability to 'bounce back' from negative experiences. In the early study of resilience, it was argued that 'special skills' may help children cope with various issues (NCH 2007). These may include individual strategies and support from schools, families and communities, and are described as resulting in good outcomes regardless of individual children's statuses. Those skills guide children's ability to cope with stress, recover from traumatic incidents and prepare for future issues. The skills discussed in the many studies on resilience focus on relationships, trust and assertiveness as well as on the more complex notions of realistic goal-settings, positive self-views and the ability to manage feelings and impulses. Some of those factors are listed by Daniel and Wassell (2002), such as having a sense of competence, a sense of control, problem-solving skills, communication skills, empathy, reflective behaviour, independence and social abilities as well as trust and access to resources. Furthermore, Werner (1993) distinguished three protective factors:

1. personal traits

2. a strong supportive family

3. the positive input of the community including peers and friends.

In my work as a clinical social worker, and despite the validity of the current research, I noticed that teachers and parents did not always have the time or opportunity to teach their children the necessary life skills to overcome all the stressors and traumas of life. A minority of children with, or at risk of, substantial issues were adequately prioritized to receive clinical support. However, a larger number of children with what may be considered 'routine' issues, some of whom lacked confidence, communication or positive-thinking skills, were not screened and consequently not supported – they were not clinically 'depressed' or 'oppositional'. The concept that resilience should be regarded as a preventative notion, teaching fundamental building blocks of skills in a systematic way to all children in routine settings, stood out to me as a current gap. Communication skills, emotional regulation, grief and loss, positive thinking, social skills and self-esteem are commonly taught in clusters throughout schools and counselling groups; a preventative programme encompassing all of those skills emerged as a potential solution.

Healthy Mindsets for Super Kids is a preventative, universal programme teaching core resilience skills to children aged 7–14 years. The programme is written in a way that allows great flexibility in its delivery. Facilitators may teach a module over the course of an hour or for up to three hours. Similarly, the worksheets and activities may be adapted for the age group of the children taught.

Two trials of the programme operated in 2011. Each intake carried a group of around ten children, with mixed genders and ages ranging from 9 to 12. Most children attended the ten sessions. Children as well as parents filled out evaluation forms and around 60 of these were returned. The trial was successful on all levels. Both parents and children involved in the programme found it beneficial and in the three months post course they felt that changes in behaviour and symptoms occurred as a result of skills taught in the modules. The mean score for the overall course was 8.9/10 from the participants and 8.6/10 from the parents. Some of the positive feedbacks related to the 'hands-on' activities at the end of each lesson, the user-friendly worksheets and lesson summaries, the holistic range of topics and the inclusion of superhero themes and the comic book.

Healthy Mindsets for Super Kids is divided into ten modules:

1. Self-Esteem

2. Communication Skills

3. Positive Thinking 1

4. Positive Thinking 2

5. Grief and Loss

6. Stress and Anxiety Management

7. Anger Management

8. Healthy Relationships 1

9. Healthy Relationships 2

10. Healthy Minds in Healthy Bodies.

Each module, illustrated with its own superhero and a comic strip representing a particular skill, contains a lesson, worksheets, interactive exercises and a 'hands-on' activity which complements the core skills discussed during the module. Introduce the background story by providing the participants with the first four comic pages and explaining the overall story during the first module. Subsequently, present each child with a comic strip of each character during every module. This has the purpose of introducing each new skill in the context of the lesson. Finally, distribute the last four pages of the comic book during the last module. This should flow and children should be encouraged to keep the whole comic together in view of reminding themselves of the story and of the skills learned.

The 'hands-on' activity may be craft, art, role-play or other creative segment. The variety of teaching medias, as well as the attractive comic strips, allow all age groups and learning styles to participate and to relate to the concepts presented in the module. Ensure, in particular, that the environment and atmosphere in your groups is conducive to learning and therapy. This may be facilitated through one-on-one debriefing, group redirection, de-escalation techniques or motivational interviewing. You should also be aware of your participants' learning styles. Younger children will possibly learn more from the 'hands-on' activities than they will discussing the worksheets. Children's literacy levels will need to be accommodated as well as individual learning styles (visual, auditory, hands-on).

Modules can be offered separately or as a whole programme, depending on the needs of the participants, facilitators or organizations. Each 'hands-on' activity segment comes with detailed instructions, material required and a clear purpose. It is recommended that you ensure the provision of tables and chairs and provide craft material and resources that are non-toxic and washable, as well as a variety of pens, crayons, stickers, collage, magazines, and so on, in a choice of unisex colours. All worksheets, activity sheets and handouts can be found within their respective session modules.

Finally, in addition to the worksheets and exercises, each lesson comes with detailed facilitator's instructions and discussion ideas. A summary of teachings is distributed by the facilitator to the participants of each lesson. This is designed to foster the involvement of parents and carers in practising the new skills at home as well as making the lesson more 'interesting'. A binding or display folder for storing their worksheets in is recommended and children should be encouraged to take pride in their work and to keep their folder in a way that promotes the review of any of the worksheets. Another suggestion concerns the comic book pages, which could be collected at the end of each module to become a full story in its own right. At the end of the course, you could suggest to the children that they colour in the comic book pages or even create their own sequel, demonstrating their ability to apply the skills they have learned to their own made-up superheroes.

Finally, a range of appendices have been included in this book for your personal use. They include examples of templates to facilitate the course, evaluation forms, promotional material, attendance certificate and sheets.

Session | 1

Self-Esteem

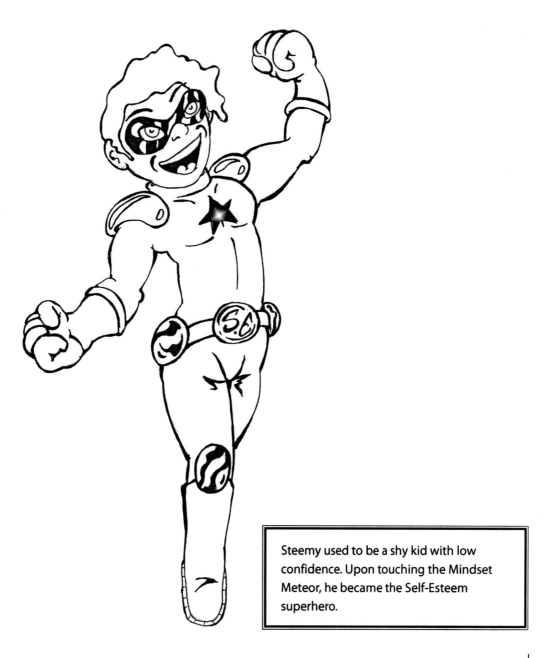

Steemy used to be a shy kid with low confidence. Upon touching the Mindset Meteor, he became the Self-Esteem superhero.

|

SESSION 1: SELF-ESTEEM MODULE

1. Welcome and introduction amongst participants

The warm and non-threatening introduction of the participants amongst themselves is vital for the group to start interacting in a positive way. Many of the children who will be involved in the programme will have self-esteem, self-confidence or communication issues. Ensuring that the introduction goes smoothly facilitates the nurturing of all children and helps their feelings to be valued in the group. Before starting the session, make sure that participants are aware of exit points and the location of the toilet. Give particular instructions relevant to your group.

Welcome the group to the *Healthy Mindsets for Super Kids* programme, a fun programme designed to teach us to think positively and learn skills to make us feel happier. Tell the children that they're going to start by introducing themselves to the group – start with yourself and then go round the circle, thanking the children after everyone has been introduced.

Introduce the children to the comic pages, explaining that *Healthy Mindsets for Super Kids* comes with its own comic book. Set the background through presenting the first four pages of the main story. Explain that a group of children, who lacked many of the skills learned in the programme, were hit by a meteor that came from a different planet. The meteor had the power to reverse negative energy into positives. So everyone who got hit became the opposite of what they were before. Introduce Steemy as a boy who lacked confidence and self-esteem. After he was hit by the meteor, he developed superhero confidence. Through this module, the children try to learn this skill too. Explain to the participants that in every module, you will provide them with comic strips. If they save them all, at the end of the programme they will have a whole superhero story.

2. Getting to know each other

This first session focuses on you and the children getting to know each other and looking at yourselves in a positive and healthy way. The first activity has a dual purpose: to act as an icebreaker and provide all children the opportunity to talk about themselves.

Sitting down as a group in a circle, spread Icebreaking Cards (found at the back of this book) on the ground and allow each child to choose a card that represents how they feel about themselves. Ask them to name one of their strengths and describe it. Assist the children in taking turns and sharing the reason they chose any particular card.

3. We are all good at different things

In this section, briefly discuss the strengths the participants have identified in themselves. Explain that we are all different – we are good at some things, and not so good at others – emphasizing that this is normal. Continue by discussing how the children may feel when someone else is better than them in particular areas (sports, school, etc.) – for example, they might feel sad, and might even forget that they're good at different things.

DISCUSSION

Has that happened to you? Have you even thought you were good at nothing because you were not good at the things your friends were good at? Get in a pair and discuss an experience you have had where you thought you were bad at something because someone you knew was better than you at it.

After the children have talked in their pairs, come back as a group and share examples.

4. Many areas in our lives

Thank all participants for sharing their thoughts and experiences, and then distribute the first worksheet of the Self-Esteem module.

WORKSHEET 1: 'I CAN DO THINGS IN MANY AREAS'

This worksheet represents a wheel of areas (i.e. academic, sports, social, spiritual, etc.). The purpose of this activity is to explore all of those areas and identify things in areas the children may enjoy or be good at. Additionally, the purpose of this worksheet is to identify that we may not be good at all areas in the wheel and that this is acceptable.

After a discussion of the different areas, helping the children to understand what each area means, assist them in filling in the blank wheel with examples in each area of things they can do or that they simply enjoy. Some children may need prompting.

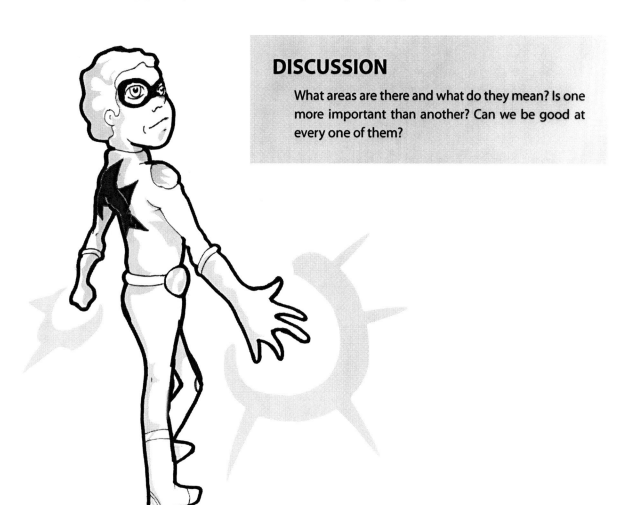

DISCUSSION

What areas are there and what do they mean? Is one more important than another? Can we be good at every one of them?

5. We all have both positives and negatives

Continue the discussion by explaining that another way to look at strengths and being OK with weaknesses is by writing them down; then distribute the second worksheet.

WORKSHEET 2: GOOD POINTS AND BAD POINTS

This worksheet is a simple list of positives and negatives. Children often find it easier to list negatives. They may need to be encouraged to identify positives and they should not be permitted to come up with more negatives than positives. To be successful, this worksheet should record no more than two-thirds of negatives compared to positives.

After the children have filled in the worksheets individually, they come back as a group to have a discussion.

DISCUSSION

We all seem to write down more weaknesses than strengths. Why is that? What does it show about how we see ourselves? How can we change this?

6. Ending activity: Positive Self-View Shirts

PURPOSE:

Participants make 'Positive Self-View Shirts' to remind themselves of their strengths and the fact that having weaknesses does not make them 'faulty'.

RESOURCES:

- white shirts

- fabric markers

- newspaper to place between layers of material (shirts).

Distribute one shirt per child (unless you have requested the children to bring their own). Participants place one layer of paper between the two layers of the shirt (as the ink may seep through). Ask the children to think of symbols, pictures or words which remind them of their strengths and positive identity. Walk among the children, prompting them if required, and sharing ideas with each individual child about their strengths based on the discussions that have taken place today and the worksheets they have filled out. The children spend the next 30 minutes drawing these ideas on their shirts with the fabric markers. Words, pictures and symbols may be used and 'freestyle' art should be encouraged. The shirts should look uplifting, positive and be unique to each child. Praise participants for their efforts and results.

7. Conclusion

Summarize the lesson and worksheets with the participants, building on what they have expressed and shared and using the points listed in the Summary.

SESSION 1:   SELF-ESTEEM
Worksheet 1
I can do things in many areas!!!

Have a look at the example wheel and give it a go!

The example wheel contains the following areas and examples:

Spiritual: Purpose, Values, Religion

Emotional / Heart: Sharing things, Emotions, Supportive

Physical: Healthy, Exercises, Sports

Family: Sharing, Team work

Fun: Talking, Projects

Academic: School, Reading, Writing, Maths, Science

Social: Friends, Communicating, Being kind, Going out

SESSION 1: SELF-ESTEEM
Worksheet 2
Good Points and Bad Points

Guess what? I have weaknesses – yeah I'm human!
  We all have good points and bad points. We want to improve our bad points for sure, but we also want to focus on our strengths! Because after all, we will never be perfect!

My negatives	My positives

SUMMARY

'I have positives and negatives – yeah I'm human!'

- I have both weaknesses and strengths.

- Everyone has both weaknesses and strengths and that's normal!

- It's OK to feel down when someone is better than us at something. However, we can focus on our own strengths to make ourselves feel good. We too are good at things!

- There is more than *one* area in our lives and we should remember to try in all of them. We cannot be good in all of these and because we are different, we will all be good in different ones.

- Being comfortable with our good points as well as our bad points is what gives us good self-esteem. Self-esteem helps us be happy and achieve loads in our lives. If you remember your good points and focus on them rather than the negatives, you will grow more self-esteem.

- Wear the shirt you have made today, as a reminder that your strengths outweigh your weaknesses and that you are special too!

WEEKLY TIP FOR PARENTS

- Remind your child of their strengths and their areas of strength whenever they are feeling down. Encourage your child to name them.

Session | 2

Communication Skills

Link always had trouble communicating... But with his new superpowers, poor communication is history!

SESSION 2: COMMUNICATION SKILLS MODULE

1. Greeting the participants

Welcome the children back for their second session. Some of them will be very excited to return while others may continue to feel uncomfortable, especially if the group did not know each other prior to the beginning of the programme. Take a few minutes to reintroduce everyone's names and facilitate friendship groups. Then summarize the previous session and ask the children what they thought about it, including what they learned, what they liked and what they didn't like. Ensure that all children have an equal opportunity to voice their thoughts in the group.

Introduce Link to the children. Link is their communication skills guru. He has a way to communicate with people in every way possible. His story will help them to learn about those ways. Present them with the comic strips about Link at this point.

2. Introductory activity

The second session of the programme focuses on communication skills, particularly assertiveness training. Not only may children not understand the concepts of 'passive', 'aggressive' and 'assertive', they may also not be familiar with the concept of 'body language' as a communicative tool. Ask the children to form a circle and start by introducing the topic of the session and introducing the notions of 'verbal and body language' using the Icebreaking Cards found at the end of this book (or any other 'feeling' cards).

Tell the children that today's session is on communication – on learning to use our bodies and our words in a way that gets us what we need, without getting in trouble – and that the same as last week, they're going to start the session by doing an activity. Explain that you are going to spread some cards on the floor and when you've finished you're going to ask all of the children to take one card that represents the way they communicate with others. They should pick a card that looks like them when they're trying to talk to someone. Tell them that they will take turns in telling the whole group why they've picked that card and anything they want to share about it at that point.

3. Communication styles

HANDOUT 1: COMMUNICATION STYLES

Distribute the first handout. This introduces the basic styles of communication (i.e. passive, aggressive and assertive) and highlights their individual features. Its purpose is to help you enter into a discussion with the children on which communication styles they recognize in themselves and other people.

DISCUSSION

Do you recognize those styles of communication? In yourself? In others? And in which way? Discuss common examples of aggressive and passive behaviour and emphasize assertiveness as being best.

ACTIVITY 1: PASSIVE, AGGRESSIVE OR ASSERTIVE?

The purpose of this activity is for the children to discover the correct communication style or behaviour featured in the scenarios. Prior to the session, make three signs on A4 sheets, as follows:

1. Aggressive (in red)

2. Assertive (in green)

3. Passive (in pale blue).

Stick these on a wall where there is room for the children to line up below the signs.

Distribute Activity Sheet 1 and ask the children to take turns reading the case scenarios, and deciding whether they wish to line up behind the red (Aggressive), green (Assertive) or pale blue (Passive) signs. Have a quick discussion about the case scenarios after each one.

DISCUSSION

Why is each example passive, aggressive or assertive? What 'gave it away'? What are the consequences of being passive or aggressive? What would be the rewards of being assertive?

4. Body language types

Now introduce the concept of body language. As stated earlier, this may be a new concept for the children and they may need some help in understanding it. Explain that there is a form of communication other than words that we sometimes forget about and this is called body language; it includes eye contact, facial expressions, our bodies, and even our hand movements. You may choose to display some obvious non-verbal cues to illustrate passive, aggressive or assertive body language.

DISCUSSION

Let's talk about body language that could look aggressive, passive or assertive. What would it look like?

ACTIVITY 2: USING BODY LANGUAGE

Simply ask the children to demonstrate a passive body language, an aggressive body language and an assertive body language. You may tell them to show a 'passive' body language on the count of three, and continue until every style of communication has been illustrated well by all the children.

5. The Magical Formula

At this point introduce the notion that some ways of talking to people are better than others and there is a 'right' formula to communicate. Now introduce the 'Magical Formula' to the group and explain that by using it, the children will achieve healthier and better results.

Start by reminding the children that there are three ways of talking to people and that when we're assertive, we respect our rights *and* the rights of others; also, we are more likely to achieve what we need by being assertive. Tell them that you are going to teach them a Magical Formula – a way to use words that will help them achieve what they need and this will allow other people to understand the true meaning behind these words. Explain that this is not a miracle solution to get the latest toy but is a better way to be understood.

WORKSHEET 1: THE MAGICAL FORMULA

Distribute the worksheet and go through it step by step with the children. As a group come up with more examples and ask the children to write two examples of their own at the bottom of the worksheet.

DISCUSSION

Why do you think the Magical Formula works? What would it mean if it didn't work? Is it still OK to be assertive if it doesn't bring you all your wishes?

6. Ending activity: Communication Role-Plays

PURPOSE:

Summarizes the learning about communication, verbal and body language and the Magic Formula. This activity merges all the skills discussed today into a role-play.

RESOURCES:

- role-play scenarios on the Ending Activity Sheet
- participants.

Role-playing can be a fun way to learn, but it can feel very daunting for some children. You should be aware of the group dynamics and be mindful of individual children's strengths and weaknesses.

With the children sitting in a circle on the floor or at a table, distribute one scenario to each child – you can do this by allowing them to choose, or by letting them randomly pick scenarios out of a hat, or by assigning a scenario to each individual participant. Children can work and role-play together, depending on the group dynamics. Give them ten minutes to prepare these 'acts' and two minutes to present them to the larger group. As part of the presentation, ask them to discuss their thoughts on the scenarios. Children should take turns at demonstrating the passive, aggressive and assertive ways of communicating. This activity should be non-threatening and entertaining. After each 'act', encourage all the children to praise their fellow group members for their efforts and to foster positive reinforcement (e.g. clapping, shaking hands, etc.).

DISCUSSION

What are your thoughts on the scenarios and how the participants used their skills? Which ones do you think would work in real life?

7. Conclusion

Summarize the lesson and the worksheets with the participants, building on what they have expressed and shared and using the points listed in the Summary.

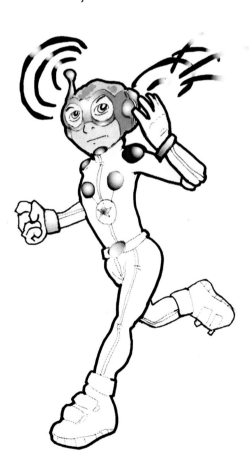

▨ SESSION 2: COMMUNICATION SKILLS
Handout 1
Communication Styles

PASSIVE	ASSERTIVE	AGGRESSIVE
• 'Shy' style	• 'Best' style	• 'Mean' style
• Does not speak his/her mind	• Speaks his/her mind, but kindly	• Forces his/her opinion onto others
• Puts the rights/needs of others in front of his/her own	• Puts the rights/needs of others at the same level as his/hers	• Puts his/her rights/needs in front of everybody else's
• Can be taken advantage of and be disrespected	• Is taken seriously and is respected	• Scares people
• May feel sad, lonely and withdrawn	• Feels good about himself/her	• May act as a bully or may not understand why he/she has few friends

|

▨ SESSION 2: COMMUNICATION SKILLS
Activity sheet 1
Passive, Aggressive, Assertive

✂ ....

'Hey, you! Can you look after my bag, I'm going to play soccer and I don't want to leave my bag unattended.'
(Someone walking past another person)

✂ ....

'Excuse me, that was my juice, but that's all right – you can drink it anyway.'
(Someone has found a carton of juice on the bench and decided to drink it)

✂ ....

'I'd like you to stop using my pencils without asking, please.'

✂ ....

✓

✂ ....

'Go away!'
(Someone tells another person to go away for no reason)

✂ ....

'You can't play with us. Go and cry to the teacher!'

✂ ....

'I'm sorry, I didn't hear what you said. Can you repeat it?'

✂ ....

'You did really well at that maths test. Well done!'

✂ ....

A person gives another person their last chocolate even though they really wanted it.

✂ ....

A friend returns your dress with a huge stain on it but you don't say anything because you're worried your friend will be angry if you make a comment.

✂ ....

'I really like it when you sing. Do you think you could sing to me right after I've finished my homework?'

✂ ....

SESSION 2: COMMUNICATION SKILLS
Worksheet 1
The Magical Formula: The Magical Way to Talk to Others!

What I need/would like... (Always use 'I' – do not blame someone else!)	Because... (A good reason will give you more than a bad one!)	Magic words... ('Please,' 'Thank you,' 'It would mean a lot to me!')	Ask if this would be OK... ('How would you feel about this?' 'Would this be OK with you?')
'I would like to go to my friend's house for a sleepover.'	'Because it's her birthday and I have finished all my homework.'	'Please, Mum/Dad.'	'Would that be OK with you?'
'Can I borrow some of your colouring pencils?'	'Because mine are all broken and used.'	'Please, John/Sarah.'	'I'll return them right away – is that OK?'
Example 1:			
Example 2:			

| 43

SESSION 2: COMMUNICATION SKILLS
Ending Activity Sheet
Role-Play Scenarios
Using The Magical Formula

✂ ....

You would like to go to a sleepover.

✂ ....

You would like a particular student at your school to stop borrowing your pens.

✂ ....

You would like your sister to stay out of your room.

✂ ....

Your brother asked to borrow a DS game that you're using.

✂ ....

You would like to have lasagne for dinner.

✂ ....

✂ ....

You would like your little cousin to stop using your make-up.

✂ ....

You would like to ask the teacher to repeat the last instructions.

✂ ....

You would like to borrow someone's shoes.

✂ ....

Someone asked you to go to a party with them but you feel too tired to go.

✂ ....

You would like to watch TV for five more minutes to see the end of the show.

✂ ....

You would like people to stop being so noisy around you because you have a headache.

✂ ....

You would like to go to the school disco.

✂ ....

You would like a particular neighbour in your street to stop throwing balls at your window.

✂ ....

You would like your brother to stop jumping on you in the swimming pool.

✂ ....

Your sister asks to borrow the phone while you're on a call.

✂ ....

✓

✂ ....

You would like to order a take-away meal for your birthday.

✂ ....

You would like your little cousin to stop following you around.

✂ ....

You would like to ask the shopkeeper to repeat how much you owe.

✂ ....

You would like to borrow someone's new release DVD movie.

✂ ....

Someone asks you to go to the movies with them but you hate the movie they have chosen.

✂ ....

You would like to give your opinion in a conversation that did not include you.

✂ ....

You would like your friends to stop swearing around you because it offends you.

✂ ....

SUMMARY

'I understand that there are different communication styles and that by using the Magical Formula I can be assertive, not passive or aggressive.'

- Communication can be passive, aggressive or assertive.

- Assertiveness is the balance between respecting others' rights with my rights.

- I want to try to be assertive as much as possible as it will help me get/keep friends and achieve what I need.

- My body language influences the way others see me.

- I will practise the role-plays and remember the differences they made!

WEEKLY TIPS FOR PARENTS

- Ask your child what the differences are between assertiveness, aggressiveness and passiveness. Remind them to be assertive when communicating around you.

- Remind your child to use the Magical Formula when communicating with you if they are struggling to be assertive.

Session | 3

Positive Thinking Part 1

Optimus' thoughts changed drastically when he received the gift of positive thinking. This superhero has a way with perceptions!

|

SESSION 3: POSITIVE THINKING MODULE 1

1. Greeting the participants

The third module of the programme on positive thinking is a core topic and is split into two parts to allow the content to be facilitated slowly and surely. Positive thinking – trying to see the good side in most things – is the basis for depression prevention in both children and adults alike. Mastering the concept of positive self-talk ensures that children are able to process information in a positive way.

By the third session, the children should be able to recognize and recall each others' names. Summarize the communication skills learned in the previous session and give the children the opportunity to ask questions or share examples of their 'successes'. Ask everyone what they thought of last week's session. What did they learn, like or dislike? How did they apply the things that were discussed in the last session and what happened?

Introduce Optimus and explain that he wasn't always so positive! Optimus used to be fairly negative, actually. Through his story, the children will learn to think positively and they will learn about this when they read his comic strip, which introduces this module on positive thinking. Provide the children with the comic strip at this point.

2. Introductory activity

Introduce the topic of positive thinking and the notion that positive self-talk has the potential to lead people to feel happier by transforming thoughts and, as a consequence, the interpretation of events. The introductory activity will involve using the Icebreaking Cards (found at the back of this book). Spread these either on the floor or on a table. Invite the children to choose a card which represents the way they routinely view things in their life (e.g. angry, scared, unsure, confident, happy, etc.). Ask whether they always view things happily, always negatively or sometimes a bit of both. Ask how they think their outlook on life is.

3. Why do I feel like this?

This part of the module explores the reasons why children may feel sad about things and introduces Cognitive Behaviour Therapy (CBT) principles published in the literature. This should be explained slowly and clearly as these concepts can be difficult for children to grasp.

HANDOUT 1: WHY DO WE FEEL SAD OR ANGRY?

Distribute the handout – this is a written summary of why we may feel the way we do. Children may be allowed to colour in the picture on the handout as it is discussed (at the discretion of the facilitator and depending on the children's developmental needs).

Explain to the children there are a few reasons why some people might feel sad about things while others may not be as sad in the same situation. The first reason may be that they have a sad way of thinking about themselves. Another reason might be that they have a sad way of looking at the events.

DISCUSSION

Do you recognize any of these reasons either in yourself or other people? When you get sad, which is your biggest problem – the way you look at things, the way you look at yourself or how you think about the future? How do you think those things affect you?

WORKSHEET 1: WHAT DOES IT MEAN TO HAVE A HAPPY VIEW OF MYSELF?

Now distribute the first worksheet, which enables the children to explore how they view themselves. It introduces the 'bright and bubbly thoughts' and the 'dark and gloomy thoughts' and how those affect Optimus, the character of this module. The purpose of this worksheet is to emphasize that prior to his transformation, Optimus had pretty negative thoughts. After the transformation, he was able to have positive ideas. Read the worksheet aloud with the group.

Ask the children to write down the way they could look at themselves, using bright and bubbly thoughts. This involves them applying the bright and bubbly thoughts *about themselves* to examples of their choice. You may prompt the children if necessary.

Tell them that we can look at ourselves in two ways: a dark and gloomy way or a bright and bubbly way.

DISCUSSION

What happened to Optimus when he was bright and bubbly? What about when he was dark and gloomy?

WORKSHEET 2: WHAT DOES IT MEAN TO HAVE A POSITIVE VIEW OF THINGS?

Now distribute the second worksheet. This introduces the 'give yourself a pat' (positive) view and the 'crawl under a mat' (negative) view of events. As with the previous worksheet, read and explain the worksheet to the group.

Explain that when things happen to us, we can see them either in a horrible way or in an exciting way, and sometimes this depends on our mood or the things we're going through; this is OK but we should practise seeing things in a way that makes us feel better. Tell the children that they are going to read about Optimus and how things didn't go to plan when his baby sister got sick.

DISCUSSION

How did Optimus look at the situation? Which situation made it better? Which situation made it worse? How do you think it differs? How would you look at the situation if you were Optimus?

Ask the children to imagine they are in Optimus' situation. They should find an example of a negative way of looking at the situation and one good way of looking at that same situation. This involves them applying the 'give yourself a pat' (positive) way of thinking *about events* to examples of their choice. You may prompt the children if necessary.

4. The 'ABC Model'

The ABC Model is a strong component of CBT and will be used and referred to in this programme. This model introduces the concept of challenging negative thoughts to become positive and teaches the children to try to find alternative thoughts to their negatives. Additionally, it attempts to show that negative thoughts bring about negative consequences while positive thoughts bring about positive consequences. This is a complex construct and should be adapted to the developmental level of children.

WORKSHEET 3: THE ABC MODEL

Distribute the third worksheet. Tell the children to think of Optimus and how he had two ways of looking at what happened to him. The first thought he had was negative and led him to feel angry and resentful. His second thought was positive and led him to feel peaceful and maybe even worried about his sister. Ask the children to choose a situation that happened to them where maybe they had negative feelings. They would write the situation down in the 'action' box on the worksheet. Then they should think of a negative thought they may have had about the situation and write it down in the 'negative thought' box. They should then try to remember whether the negative thought brought on a negative consequence and write that down too. Finally, they should make up a positive thought and observe a positive consequence.

DISCUSSION

How do you feel about this exercise? Do you think it can actually work? What would happen if you were able to practise it every time you have negative thoughts?

Support the children in practising the ABC Model and finding new thoughts that would lead to positive and happy consequences. Children often struggle with coming up with examples and so you may choose to demonstrate an example with the whole group or with smaller groups of participants until they are able to master the exercise on their own.

5. Ending activity: Vision Boards

PURPOSE:

To allow the children to become creative and create vision boards which bring hope, happiness and excitement to them.

RESOURCES:

- old newspapers
- magazines
- stickers
- coloured paper
- cards
- felt pens
- crayons
- craft glue
- scissors
- large sheets of coloured cardboard/paper to use as vision boards.

Scatter the resources on large tables. The materials should be varied and attractive to children. Instruct the participants to sit around the tables and explain the purpose of the activity. Once the children have understood that they are to prepare an uplifting vision board for themselves, they may start the activity. Children may select images, words cut out of newspapers and magazines or draw/write pictures and words that inspire positive ideas and goals for themselves. You may assist the children with ideas or prompt them if required. The vision board should be uplifting and representative of positive thoughts. Children should be encouraged to hang out the vision board in a place where they will be able to see it regularly (e.g. their bedroom). Children should be praised and rewarded for effort and participation.

6. Conclusion

Summarize the lesson and the worksheets with the participants, building on what they have expressed and shared and using the points listed in the Summary.

SESSION 3: POSITIVE THINKING PART 1
Handout 1
Why Do We Feel Sad or Angry?

Let's start with why some children feel sad. There are a few reasons children may be sad about 'little' things:

1. They have a sad view of themselves (e.g. 'I am fat', 'I'm not clever').

2. They have a sad view of the things that happened to them (e.g. 'This is so terrible', 'This is the worst thing that could ever have happened').

If this is the case, then we could reverse this and assume that happy people are happy because:

1. They have a happy view of themselves (e.g. 'I am smart at maths/singing', 'I did my best and that's OK').

2. They have a happy view of events (e.g. 'It's not the end of the world', 'It could have been much worse – I should be grateful').

SESSION 3:   POSITIVE THINKING PART 1
Worksheet 1
What Does It Mean to Have a Happy View of Myself?

Imagine that there were two of you. One of you was so dark and gloomy it wasn't funny and the other you was bright and bubbly. Which one would you be and which one would make you feel better?

Let's see how Optimus' 'two sides' felt about themselves.

Optimus – dark and gloomy: 'I'm so stupid. I screwed up that football game. I mean, I always screw up everything at sports anyway. I'll never be good at anything. I should just start eating out of the rubbish bin or something…'

Optimus – bright and bubbly: 'I'm a pretty cool dude even though I'm not perfect! I like how I wrote that story with pictures and everything. I am proud of myself… I rock!'

How do you think Optimus felt when he was dark and gloomy, and bright and bubbly? Which one made him feel better?

What about you? How do you talk about yourself? How does it make you feel? Can you try to replace the dark and gloomy side with the bright and bubbly one? Write your name and practise in the space below:

(Your name) _____ *is bright and bubbly:* . . . .

. . . .

. . . .

. . . .

. . . .

. . . .

. . . .

. . . .

. . . .

SESSION 3:   POSITIVE THINKING PART 1
Worksheet 2
What Does It Mean to Have a Positive View of Things?

As we've seen before, there are two ways of seeing things: the happy way (AKA the 'positive way') and the sad way (AKA the 'negative way').

Let's have a look at how Optimus' two sides feel about something that happened to him. Optimus had organized with his friends to meet up after school and play a soccer game. At the last minute, his baby sister got really sick and his mother was unable to take him. Optimus had to miss out on the game for the day.

How did he look at the situation?

Optimus 'crawled under the mat' and said: 'This is the worst thing that could have happened to me. I'd rather be dead with my dog, my cat and my pet octopus! My friends will laugh at me and I hate my mum and my sister. I bet Mum's just making excuses because she doesn't want to take me!'

Optimus 'gave himself a pat' and said: 'OK, this pretty much sucks… I might not look silly though. Although it sucks, I know Mum isn't making excuses, and whining is only going to make the situation worse for me and her. I hope my baby sister gets better soon.'

What about you? Can you practise looking at things in the two ways and see which one would make you feel better? Imagine *you* are in Optimus' situation – find a negative and then a positive way of looking at the situation and write them down in the spaces opposite.

✓

(Your name) _____ *'crawled under the mat'*: ....

....

....

....

....

....

....

....

....

(Your name) _____ *'gave him/herself a pat'*: ....

....

....

....

....

....

....

....

....

SESSION 3: POSITIVE THINKING PART 1
Worksheet 3
ABC Model

We learned that we can choose to be 'bright and bubbly' like Optimus Let's practise finding alternatives to our sad thoughts. In the negative thought box we'll write the sad ending and then in the positive thought box we'll swap it for a happy ending ☺.

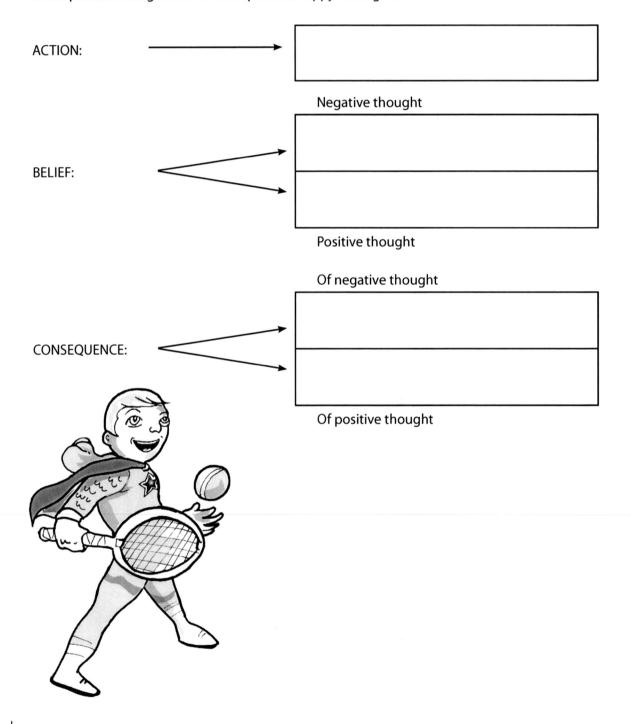

ACTION: ⟶

Negative thought

BELIEF:

Positive thought

Of negative thought

CONSEQUENCE:

Of positive thought

SUMMARY

'Positive thinking – yes, it can make me happier!'

- Happy people are happy because they have a positive view of themselves, look at things in a positive way or imagine their future in a great way!

- Challenging my thoughts and trying to turn negative thinking into positive thinking can make a big difference to how I feel!

- Remember the 'nasty thoughts' and how they can trick us into believing negative things. Always challenge them!

- Find alternatives to negatives. Challenge, challenge and challenge until you find a better thought.

- If you feel negative or sad, try to find someone you can talk to and share your thinking with them.

WEEKLY TIPS FOR PARENTS

- Do an ABC Model exercise together and discuss. Ask your child questions about 'negative' thoughts. Try to recognize them in yourselves or other people and discuss.

- If your child is being negative, remind them to do the ABC Model and to challenge the negative into becoming a positive. Help them find positive alternatives at the beginning.

Session | 4

Positive Thinking Part 2

SESSION 4: POSITIVE THINKING MODULE 2

1. Greeting the participants and introductory activity

Welcome the children back for their fourth session. This is a follow-up from last week's module. Ensure that children have started to grasp the concepts of positive thinking and allow any questions or clarification to occur. Additionally, take a few minutes to debrief on the application of the skills taught last week through examples, and to facilitate the group's socialization. Go around the circle asking everyone to give one example of how they changed something negative into something positive this week. Ask them to give an example of how they challenged a thought, and to try to explain how it happened.

2. WWW (What Worked Well today!)

EXERCISE 1: WWW (WHAT WORKED WELL TODAY!)

This exercise involves each child finding *one* thing that worked well for them today, no matter how small this event might be. It could be a yummy treat for lunch, an 'A' for a piece of homework, or the bus being on time. Some children who may have got into a habit of thinking negatively may find this exercise complex at first. If this is the case give examples and assist any children who are struggling. You may choose to pair children up if appropriate. Encourage the children to practise WWW daily or as often as possible to help them focus on the positives, and also encourage the parents to practise it as a family.

DISCUSSION

What worked well for you today? What if nothing appears to have worked well? How can WWW make us feel better?

3. Best, worst and realistic case scenarios

This part of the module is designed to help children practise thinking about best and worst case scenarios and to settle for the more realistic example. Explain that we usually imagine things to be worse than they are in reality and when we practise looking at things as a realistic case scenario, it helps us to see things in a more positive light.

ACTIVITY 2: WHAT DO YOU THINK COULD HAPPEN?

Start by recapping how the last two modules have explored how we can sometimes get a bit negative and how it's important to challenge our thoughts into becoming positives. Tell the children that today they are going to talk about best, worst and realistic case scenarios. They should imagine that they were being silly with their friends at school and were given a detention for doing cartwheels on the concrete. In this situation what do they think their parents would say or do?

DISCUSSION

What would be the worst thing that could happen? How would you feel if you thought about it?

What would be the best thing that could happen? How would you feel if you thought about that version?

Now, what would be the most likely thing to happen – the closest to reality, without being too dramatic or not dramatic enough? What would be the realistic case scenario and how would you feel about thinking about this outcome as opposed to the other two?

Which one would be better to imagine and why? How can we learn always to look at the realistic scenarios and not the worst/best case scenarios?

ACTIVITY 3: FINDING THE WORST, BEST AND REALISTIC CASE SCENARIO

This exercise is designed to provide a further opportunity for the children to practise the 'best, worst and realistic case scenarios'. Using the Activity 3 sheet, ask the children to form groups of two or three. Give each group a different case scenario and ask them to discuss the worst case scenario, the best one and then the realistic scenario within their small groups. After an appropriate amount of time, the large group re-forms and the children discuss the scenarios together. Make sure that all children have the opportunity to practise and foster their confidence by speaking up in front of the group.

4. Evidence boards

WORKSHEET 1: MY EVIDENCE BOARD

Distribute the first worksheet to the children. This entails writing a statement in the middle of the page in the space provided and finding evidence of its truth or inaccuracy (e.g. 'I am stupid' or 'I am pretty'), and writing as many examples as possible to engender a positive conclusion.

An example might be to write the statement 'I am stupid' and add evidence of its inaccuracy such as 'I got an "A" at school', 'I made a cake by myself', 'I can navigate the computer' and so on.

Prior to letting the children attempt the worksheet on their own, prepare them as a group by telling them that we all have times when we think sadly or negatively and that an Evidence Board is a good way of learning to challenge ourselves with evidence or proof that we are good, smart or that things are going well. Give the children the example of Optimus who failed a maths test and thought he was really stupid and tell them that his mother made him do an Evidence Board. At this point you may use a whiteboard to show the children what this would look like. Write 'Optimus is smart' (as you are trying to convince him that he is) and ask the children to find as much proof as possible that he is.

Make sure that all children at least attempt the worksheet and help them to find their own examples and 'evidences'.

DISCUSSION

How easy or hard was this exercise? How do you feel about it? Do you believe that it could actually work?

5. Ending activity: Feel-Good Exercise

PURPOSE:

To foster a feeling of individual self-worth and a sense of belonging in the group.

RESOURCES:

- one sheet of paper for each participant (coloured or printed paper may be nicer to use if available)
- Ending Activity Sheet – A4 printing paper may suffice
- pens and felt pens.

Having printed individual pieces of paper with the names of individual children on them and spread them on tables, ask each child to think of one positive message to say about each participant in the group. You may wish to spend some time reinforcing group rules (e.g. being friendly and polite and giving appropriate versus inappropriate messages). Each participant is required to go around the room and write one positive thing on each fellow participant's sheet of paper. You should monitor that everyone receives the same amount of positive comments and check the appropriateness of comments written by walking with the children around the table. Give praise and positive reinforcement during this time. The sheets are given to their rightful owner at the end of the session.

6. Conclusion

Summarize the lesson and the worksheets with the participants, building on what they have expressed and shared and using the points listed in the Summary.

SESSION 4: POSITIVE THINKING PART 2
Activity 3
Finding the Worst, Best and Realistic Case Scenario

Ask the children to find the different scenarios as a pair or in a threesome in the case study they're given:

✂ ....

1. Your mother told you that you weren't allowed to take your birthday money (£20) to school but you did anyway. At home time, you realize that someone has stolen your wallet.
Find the worst case scenario, the best case scenario and the realistic case scenario.

✂ ....

2. You've been invited to a sleepover at a friend's house. Then your friend tells you that you can't come any more because he/she's invited too many people.
Find the worst case scenario, the best case scenario and the realistic case scenario.

✂ ....

3. You hate maths/English and you have avoided doing your homework. However, you've just found out that your teacher spoke to your mum or dad about it and you are freaked out!
Find the worst case scenario, the best case scenario and the realistic case scenario.

✂ ....

4. You've been invited to a Halloween party and are dressed up as a ghost. When you arrive, you can see three other ghosts already there.
Find the worst case scenario, the best case scenario and the realistic case scenario.

✂ ....

5. Your teacher asked your whole class to read a huge book by the end of term. You read a page and fell asleep, it was so boring. What would you do, how would you feel?
Find the worst case scenario, the best case scenario and the realistic case scenario.

✂ ....

SESSION 4: POSITIVE THINKING PART 2
Worksheet 1
My Evidence Board

Write something in the circle (e.g. 'I am smart', 'I am special', 'I am not selfish', etc.). Find and write down as much evidence as you can to prove it!

SESSION 4:   POSITIVE THINKING PART 2
Ending Activity Sheet
Feel-Good Exercise

....

(Name of participant)

SUMMARY

'Positive thinking – yes, it can make me happier!'

- Refresh yourself with what we learned last week (ABC Model and positive thinking).

- What are best, worst and realistic case scenarios? Which one is best and how do you practise thinking realistically?

- WWW stands for 'What Worked Well' today. Ask your family if you could all do WWW together – at the dinner table, before bed, in the car or any suitable time.

- Remember the feel-good exercise. Tell others nice things and accept their compliments back!

- Do an Evidence Board regularly, especially when crazy thoughts creep in or you're just feeling low. Teach your family about them.

WEEKLY TIPS FOR PARENTS

- Ask your child questions about the Evidence Board, the best, worst and realistic case scenarios and WWW.

- If possible, get them to draw you an Evidence Board and challenge them with a realistic case scenario every time they are being dramatic.

- Try to adopt the WWW daily or regularly with the whole family. This will instil a positive thinking routine for everyone.

Session | 5

Grief and Loss

Angel and her magic butterflies now assist all children in the world to understand and walk the grief journey... After all, grief is a normal part of life.

|

SESSION 5: GRIEF AND LOSS MODULE

1. Greeting the participants

Welcome the children back for their fifth session. Give the participants an opportunity to share their 'successes' or 'attempts' at practising the positive thinking skills. Encourage the children and reward any attempts, no matter how insignificant. Children should be prompted to praise each other and show team attitude.

This module has been designed as a 'soft' lesson on grief and loss. You should be mindful that some children will have experienced intense grief and may struggle emotionally with the topic. Other children, who have never experienced grief, may need assistance in finding examples. An opportunity to debrief on an individual basis should be offered to children who may appear upset.

Introduce the character Angel. Angel is a young girl who lost her dog recently; she loved him very much. After the meteor hit her, her magic butterflies gave her, and everyone else who felt grief, the power to heal. In this session, the children will learn about losses and how to live with them. Provide the children with her comic strip now.

2. Introduction to grief and loss

Introduce the topic of grief and loss and explain to the children that grief does not have to involve death. Grief is what we go through when we lose something or someone we really wanted or cared about, such as when someone dies or our parents divorce. However, we can experience grief in many other situations – for example, when we realize that since Dad lost his job, we won't be getting an iPod; or when we change schools; or when a friend decides not to hang out with us any more. Some children may need help in understanding the words 'grief' and 'loss'. Help participants to find different and relevant examples of grief that children may naturally experience. Introduce the first worksheet.

WORKSHEET 1: GRIEF AND LOSS

Children are asked to identify a time and a situation in their life where they felt grief; for example, maybe when a pet or family member died; maybe when they changed schools or a friend stopped being their friend; maybe when they realized that their parents could not afford to buy them the bike they had talked about. Give the children a few minutes for reflection and sharing and then tell them to write this event in the circle on the worksheet surrounded by all the emotions they felt during the loss, including negative and positive emotions. They may comment on how other people reacted as well. After the completion of the worksheet, ensure that all children's emotional needs are met.

DISCUSSION

What emotions did you feel? Did they make you feel nice or bad? How did other people around you react? How did those emotions change over time? Did you ever feel those emotions at another time for a different loss?

3. Grief Feelings

HANDOUT 1: GRIEF FEELINGS

Continue by normalizing the emotions and grief experiences the children went through by referring back to the first worksheet where children expressed similar emotions and reactions. Discuss the experiences and waves of emotions children would have experienced through their grief. In addition, explain that not everyone goes through the same feelings and that grief is now known to be very unique to each individual person. Distribute the first handout which summarizes some of the common grief feelings. The children do not write on this worksheet but participate in a discussion around possible stages. Tell the children that some people find it helpful to understand these feelings, as it helps them understand that things will get better.

DISCUSSION

Have you ever felt grief, do you think? Do you recognize those feelings in yourself or someone else? What helped you? What made it worse? What if a friend or a family member were grieving – what could you do to help?

ACTIVITY 1: BRAINSTORMING

On a whiteboard, brainstorm all the things that could make you feel better if you were grieving. Allow all children to present ideas and ensure that all participants feel included and able to contribute. Provide suggestions if the children require assistance with ideas.

Some of the things you may suggest could be:

- Talking to a grown-up the children trust about how they're feeling.

- Breathing deeply – this could be demonstrated by asking the children to stand up and walk around the room practising deep breathing.

- Writing in a journal – explain the benefits of writing down thoughts. Remind the children that it is important to finish with something happy or hopeful.

- Colouring-in sheets – art is good for releasing emotions, especially when grieving. All forms of arts are beneficial.

WORKSHEET 2: WHO CAN I TALK TO ABOUT MY FEELINGS?

Distribute the second worksheet to the children. This involves drawing their hand (five fingers) in the square and finding at least one person's name to write on each finger. More can be added if children wish to. Those individuals should be trustworthy and safe adults to talk to if the child is feeling sad or in danger. Explain that talking to someone can make the sad feelings go away. Emphasize the importance of talking about thoughts to someone responsible. You may choose to provide the children with online/phone counselling numbers.

4. Ending activity: Colouring-in Art

PURPOSE

For the children to engage in and appreciate the art of colouring on. Additionally, to utilize colouring in as an emotional regulation tool and therapeutic self-soothing strategy.

RESOURCES

- colouring-in sheets
- felt pens, crayons or paint.

Provide all children with the colouring-in sheets. More samples can be found on the internet or you may choose to use colouring-in sheets appropriate to the developmental level of participants. Ask the children to sit individually or in small groups. This activity should be peaceful and quiet and engender a relaxed feeling. Remind the children to keep a relaxed body language and to let their emotions flow. This should be a portal for grief and loss emotions to become acceptable. Allow children to colour in while discussing their emotions and thoughts, and encourage them always to find a quiet time when upset to release their feelings in a safe and healthy way. The colouring-in sheets are a freestyle activity and there is no 'right' or 'wrong' way to fill them in. Continue praising the children for their work.

5. Conclusion

Summarize the lesson and the worksheets with the participants, building on what they have expressed and shared and using the points listed in the Summary.

SESSION 5: GRIEF AND LOSS
Worksheet 1
Grief and Loss

Think about a time when you experienced grief. In the circle below write what you lost (e.g. a pet, a relative, changed school, parents divorced, a toy or particular item).

Then around the circle, write the emotions and feelings you felt (e.g. sadness, anger, curiosity, relief).

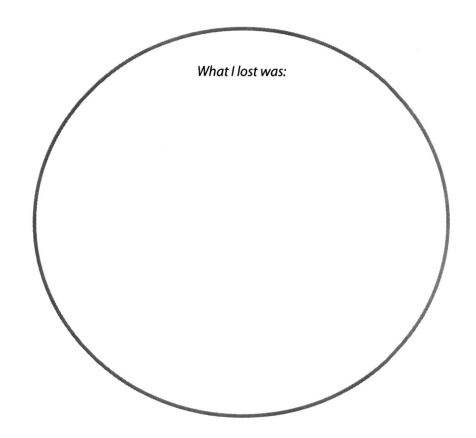

What I lost was:

|

✓

SESSION 5: GRIEF AND LOSS
Handout 1
Grief Feelings

Here are some of the emotions you may go through after experiencing grief. You may not experience them all nor experience them in any particular order, and this is normal too.

Shock
WHAT???? (What do you mean…what happened?)

Anger
I am angry at you and everyone else… It's not fair!!

Sadness
You may cry a lot and at random times.

Acceptance
I'm OK about… It was sad but things will get better.

Sometimes we may also experience:

Guilt
It's my fault. I did…and that's why…happened.

Fear
Whatever happened to…may happen to me. I used to think everything would be OK but now I'm scared. Things may not be OK after all ☹.

SESSION 5: GRIEF AND LOSS
Worksheet 2
Who Can I Talk to About My Feelings?

Draw your hand on this page.

For each finger write one person who you are comfortable talking to about your feelings.

| 81

www.clickncolour.com

www.clickncolour.com

SUMMARY

'There are many things I can grieve: from the loss of a pet or a relative to the loss of a friendship, the divorce of parents or going to a new school.'

- Emotions are normal and it's OK to have them.

- There are a number of emotions children may experience as part of their grief and for children they are mainly shock, anger and sadness, but some children may also feel guilty/shameful or afraid for the future. Finally whilst grief is a lot of work, people usually learn to live with their grief and adapt well to the new situation.

- There are some things to help you or others who are grieving around you: be nice to yourself, take deep breaths, talk to someone who cares and who can help, write in your journal and do some art activities.

WEEKLY TIPS FOR PARENTS

- Your child may be a little bit upset by today's session because we discussed grief and how we lived some of our losses. Be gentle and ask your child about how they are feeling and whether they'd like to talk about anything. Remind them that grief is normal and that after feeling sad, we start to feel better.

- Remind your child about the journal writing exercises and art activity and suggest that they write/draw daily (especially if your child is uptight/upset for any reason at a later stage).

Session | 6

Stress and Anxiety Management

The anxiety that Zen felt before the Mindset meteor hit the playground that day was paralysing. He couldn't do much without feeling sick. Now he is the guru of peace and calmness…

|

SESSION 6: STRESS AND ANXIETY MANAGEMENT MODULE

1. Greeting the participants and introduction to the session

Welcome the children back for their sixth session. This session marks the second half of the programme and healthy, closer dynamics will start to emerge in most cases. Take this opportunity to foster deeper conversations and assess whether it is appropriate to challenge and push the participants a little further. As usual, you should take a few minutes to debrief on the application of the skills taught in the last session and facilitate socialization. Additionally, due to the emotional nature of the previous session on grief and loss, you should ensure the emotional safety of the children.

Next, introduce the topic of stress and anxiety management. Many of the children attending the programme will have suffered with anxiety at some point. Others may need prompting to understand what the term 'anxiety' refers to. In your introduction clarify with the children whether they understand what anxiety means and how it can affect someone – this should be done in a non-threatening way and the terminology must be 'user friendly'. Allow everyone to take a turn at asking questions.

Introduce the character for this module as Zen, a boy who was so anxious he would make himself physically sick before stressful events happened. Ask the children whether they relate to this and subsequently introduce the comic strip to introduce Zen's story and how the meteor helped him.

2. Anxiety information

HANDOUT 1: WHAT IS ANXIETY?

Distribute handout. Go round the group letting everyone have a turn reading out one symptom. Make sure that all the children understand what the symptoms are and allow discussion around the topic as they read. The children are not required to write anything but you may allow them to colour in the sheet if this helps with keeping their attention.

3. Anxiety-coping strategies

WORKSHEET 1: THINGS I CAN DO TO HELP IF I'M FEELING ANXIOUS OR STRESSED...

Now introduce the first worksheet, which stimulates children in thinking about things that could help them if they are feeling stressed or anxious. The worksheet provides a list of suggestions which the group discusses as someone reads them out. You may choose to get the children practising some of these suggestions (deep breathing, getting a drink, counting to ten, visualizing positive things, etc.). This should be done within a team spirit and the children should be encouraged to support each other. Once the group has discussed and attempted the suggestions, the children should take a few minutes individually to find personal suggestions that would help them during an anxiety attack – this involves the children reflecting and writing on the worksheet.

ACTIVITY 1: RELAXATION EXERCISE

This exercise is a visualization/relaxation exercise. Most of the children will never have participated in anything like this and may feel awkward to begin with. You should ensure that the group is positive and feel comfortable 'giving it a go'. Continue by explaining to the participants that when children are stressed or anxious they tense their bodies up, but relaxing their bodies may help in reducing their anxiety. Next, invite the children to participate in the relaxation exercise. With the children sitting on the floor and enough space between them so they can lie down at the end of the exercise, read the Relaxation Exercise Script to them.

WORKSHEET 2: EMOTIONAL RELEASE EXERCISE

Distribute the second worksheet. This exercise involves asking the children to think of a situation that caused them anxiety or stress. You should guide the children in finding examples that do not provoke unmanageable anxiety for the participants. Appropriate suggestions might be: the first day of the *Healthy Mindsets for Super Kids* programme, attending a school camp or sleeping over at a friend's house.

Now ask the children to close their eyes and try to 'feel' this emotion again – what colour represents it? When they have decided, they should mark the appropriate square on the worksheet with their chosen colour. Continue by asking the children to think of the shape that represents the emotion they are feeling and to draw that in the appropriate square. Next, ask them to draw a picture and finally help them to find a word that represents what is bothering them or triggering their anxiety, based on the colour, shape and picture they have chosen. You can then discuss with the children the perceptions that led them to pick particular emotions and colours to represent their feelings. The purpose of this exercise is to assist the children in breaking down their emotions from a 'blurry' feeling to a descriptive word. Children may need assistance throughout this process.

DISCUSSION

Did breaking down your feeling into colour, shape and picture help you understand and name it? Is it easier to make the emotion disappear, once you know what it is?

WORKSHEET 3: STRESS FACTORS

This worksheet involves identifying the external and internal factors affecting our stress levels. While this is a fairly simple exercise, some children may still need prompting to come up with appropriate examples. You should continue to encourage the participants and praise them for their efforts. The answers should be adapted to the children's ages and developmental stages. In order to undertake this task, the children should again think of a situation where they felt anxious or stressed. This may or may not be the same example used in previous worksheets. Children should be assisted in identifying some of the contributing internal and external factors (such as being hungry, being late, having a headache, hot weather, crowded bus, etc.). You can then discuss strategies to address those factors.

DISCUSSION

Can you recognize some internal and external factors? How did they affect you? How could you change those next time?

4. Ending activity: Journal Writing

PURPOSE:

To facilitate emotional release in the children and to teach them to verbalize their thoughts.

RESOURCES:

- a journal for each child (you may provide these or request that the participants bring their own)
- stickers to decorate the pages
- glitter pens
- pencils
- markers
- glue sticks.

Prepare the tables in advance, spreading the resources within equal reach of all participants, and before the session glue a little note with each child's name and suggestions of exercises into the front cover of the journals. This will assist with making the activity more personal. (Samples of notes can be found on the Ending Activity Sheet.) Begin by reminding of previous exercises such as the 'WWW', 'Best, worst and realistic case scenarios' and ABC Model. Encourage them to use their journals to record some of those processes. As journals are distributed, explain to the children the importance of releasing emotions in a healthy and non-threatening way. Next, introduce journal writing as a strategy. Encourage the children to write down their thoughts, emphasizing positive thinking, and to practise the suggested exercises (WWW, ABC Model and Best, Worst and Realistic Case Scenarios). Assist the children in developing the ability to write in their journal and encourage them to feel confident doing so. You should continue to monitor appropriate positive writing which uplifts and helps combat anxiety. You may wish to provide the children with a couple of stickers each to take home so that they can initiate the activity continuing from home.

5. Conclusion

Summarize the lesson and the worksheets with the participants, building on what they have expressed and shared and using the points listed in the Summary.

SESSION 6:   STRESS AND ANXIETY MANAGEMENT
Handout 1
What Is Anxiety?

The word 'anxiety' refers to an unpleasant feeling with signs of worry, fear, distress and awkwardness. All children experience fears and anxiety as they grow and develop – it is very normal. Sometimes these feelings happen in specific places or about specific things, or the anxiety may be quite general.

What are some of the symptoms and signs of anxiety?

Anxiety comes with some *physical* symptoms. This is because the body has a 'flight or fight' mechanism and the brain releases a hormone called 'adrenaline'. These signs include:

- sore belly
- going to the toilet often
- dry mouth
- rapid heartbeat or palpitations
- tightness or pain in chest
- problems breathing
- dizziness
- sweating
- feelings of choking
- chills/hot flushes.

Anxiety may also come with *psychological* symptoms and these include:

- problems sleeping
- anger
- concentration problems
- feeling unreal and not in control of your actions
- fear of dying.

Children who are stressed and anxious may cry, have tantrums, freeze, cling onto a parent or withdraw from social situations with unfamiliar people.

✓

SESSION 6: STRESS AND ANXIETY MANAGEMENT
Worksheet 1
Things I Can Do to Help if I'm Feeling Anxious or Stressed...

- Take deep breaths.

- Count to 10 or 20 or as long as you need to.

- Make fun of what you're afraid/worried about.

- Go for a walk, even around the yard if need be.

- Do physical exercises.

- Have a drink of water.

- Do the ABC Model (find a positive alternative thought).

- Talk to someone you trust.

- Write in a diary or journal.

- Do something relaxing such as drawing, singing, dancing, playing a game or having a bubble bath.

Add your own now:

- ....

- ....

- ....

- ....

SESSION 6: STRESS AND ANXIETY MANAGEMENT
Activity 1
Relaxation Exercise Script

Introduction

Today we're going to practise some special kinds of exercises called relaxation exercises. These are designed to help us relax and to learn how our body feels when it is tensed and then when it is relaxed. To benefit from these exercises, you must listen to the instructions and try your best to follow the rules. Are you ready? Let's give it a go.

I want you to imagine that you have arrived on a desert island. It is peaceful, it is beautiful and you are very warm and fuzzy. You are lying on the warm sand, relaxing.

Hands and arms

You're being really relaxed and you're playing with the warm sand on the beach. You decide to grab a handful of sand and squeeze it really hard. Your hands are tight, your fists are strong, that sand cannot escape. Now let it go…let the sand fall out of your hand and rest on the beach again. Did you feel how your hands felt? Let's try again… Grab a huge handful of sand and squeeze it as hard as you can for as long as you can… Well done. Let it go now.

Arms and shoulders

You are still very relaxed on the beach but you are getting very thirsty. There is a coconut tree right above your head and you want to drink some of the milk from the coconuts. It's high and so you stretch your arms as high as you can…very high…make those arms strong…come on, reach for that coconut… Well done, you got it! Now you can have a nice drink…You would like another drink! So off you go, reach out for another coconut. Reach high, stretch those arms and make them strong… Did you reach one? You can relax again now. That feels good, doesn't it?

Jaw

You are loving this beach, listening to the sound of waves coming and going. This is so peaceful… Watch out, a wave is coming towards you. Close your mouth, clench your jaw, don't let the water get in your mouth! Well done, the wave has gone… Oh no, it's back, watch out! Close your mouth, quick! Clench your teeth and jaw…don't let the water get in! Well done, it's gone for good. How did it feel to be tense and then relaxed?

Stomach

You are still on the beach but now you are trying to fall asleep. You've woken up some monkeys by getting the coconut off the tree. They are not happy! They are about to throw coconuts at you. My goodness, watch out! Make your stomach very hard, as hard as you can. Coconuts are about to hit you! Oh no, they're not stopping…more are coming, make your stomach as hard as a rock! Well done, the monkey went away. How did it feel when your stomach was tense?

Legs and feet

You're finally at peace and trying to go back to sleep on the warm, wet sand. Something is tickling you. What is it? Oh no…tiny little crabs have landed on the beach and they are trying to come between your toes. Clench your toes, make them wiggle, try to shoo the little crabs away… I think it's working…you can stop… Oh no, I was wrong…they are back; millions of tiny crabs are trying to slip between your toes. Wiggle your toes, make them go away… Well done, they're gone for good!

Conclusion

Stay as relaxed as you can. Enjoy the sun and the sand. Remember how your body hurt when it was tense and how good it felt when it was relaxed? You can now practise relaxing your body anywhere and anytime. Slowly, open your eyes and wiggle your hands and toes. When you're ready you can sit up again.

✓

SESSION 6: **STRESS AND ANXIETY MANAGEMENT**
Worksheet 2
Emotional Release Exercise

Colour	Shape
Picture	Word

|

Worksheet 3
Stress Factors

I am stressed out...what is my problem?

What's going on physically with me?
(Am I hungry, tired, sick?)

....

....

....

What's going on around me?
(Is it noisy, crowded, hot?)

....

....

....

Do I have something on my mind?

....

....

....

DATE: ....

EVENT: ....

THOUGHTS: ....

Many factors can impact on how we react to stress. Knowing about these helps us control stress!

SESSION 6: STRESS AND ANXIETY MANAGEMENT
Ending Activity Sheet
Journal Writing

This journal belongs to ....

Some of the exercises you could
practise include:

1. The ABC Model.

2. WWW (What Worked Well today).

3. Best, Worst and Realistic Case Scenarios.

4. Find and write three things that you're looking forward to tomorrow.

5. Lots and lots of bright and bubbly thoughts.

Healthy Mindsets for Super Kids Programme

SUMMARY

'Anxiety and stress management for kids!'

- Anxiety and stress are not very nice feelings and they can make us think something is wrong with our bodies.

- We can talk to ourselves in our own minds to challenge our negative thoughts (e.g. Why are you anxious? Can you challenge this?).

- Relaxing your body can help in controlling your anxiety and stress. Practise those relaxation exercises on your own.

- We came up with a list of things you could do when you get anxious/stressed. Practise the things you wrote on the list.

- Remember the Emotion Release Exercise for the times where you're not sure as to why you're stressed or anxious.

- Remember to write down your thoughts and practise your exercises in your journal as often as you can.

WEEKLY TIPS FOR PARENTS

- If possible, ask your child to show you the relaxation exercise we did and maybe practise with them.

- Encourage your child to challenge their thoughts and to find positives when feeling anxious (e.g. 'Maybe it will be fun if I give it a go', 'I can do this').

- Encourage your child to write in their journal as often as possible and to write about 'WWW' and the 'ABC Model' (from a few sessions ago) and about their general positive feelings.

- Have a read of the tip sheets for parents from Kids Helpline (or other children's counselling helplines) and see if you can use some of it if applicable.

Session | 7

Anger Management

KK (KipKool) had serious issues with keeping Kool around other people. When the meteor struck, he became a new person. His power: to manage his anger and to teach this skill around the world.

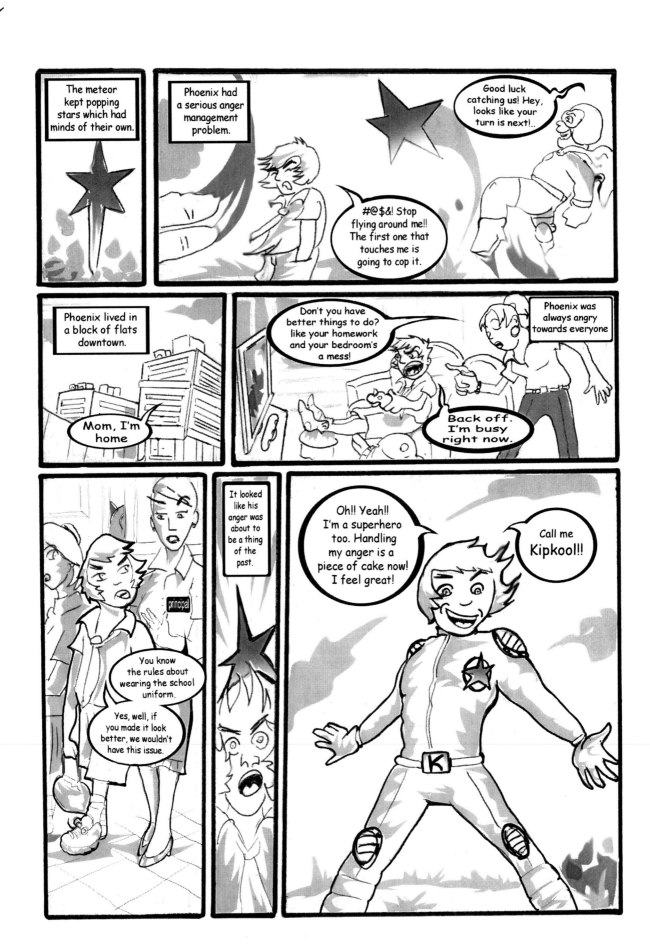

| Copyright © Stephanie Azri 2013

SESSION 7: ANGER MANAGEMENT MODULE

1. Greeting the participants and introduction to the session

The seventh session of the programme focuses on anger management skills. These are important for children to learn, as many children who display poor communication skills also struggle with frustration and anger management. This may stem from their inability to communicate their needs or problems, coping with peer, school or family issues or personality tendencies. This module will teach children about anger, and normalize the emotion as well as teach them skills to deal with it in a positive and constructive manner.

Welcome the children back and take a few minutes to debrief on the application of the skills taught in the last module and to facilitate socialization. You may invite children to share examples of how they combatted anxiety and stress using the previous exercises. Now introduce the topic of anger management and verify the children's understanding of both anger and anger management. Allow everyone to take a turn.

Introduce KipKool at this point. Explain that KipKool was a fairly aggressive child; the type of boy who always got into trouble and who forgot to be respectful at times. When the meteor hit him, his new superpower was to be able to manage his anger. He was suddenly able to calm down. Emphasize this skill as something all participants will learn through this module and hand out KipKool's comic strip.

2. What is anger?

Invite all the children to participate in an activity using the Icebreaking Cards (found at the back of the book). Ask them to pick a card that represents how they act when they get angry. Going around the group, offer all children the opportunity to show their card and say why they chose it.

HANDOUT 1: WHAT IS ANGER?

On completion of the first activity, introduce the first handout. The children may take turns in reading parts of the worksheet. As it is being read, engage the group in discussion. Ensure that all the children understand and explain any difficult words if necessary. Ensure that all children understand and explain any diffcult words if necessary.

DISCUSSION

Do you think it is OK to get angry? Do you behave differently in different situations? How does anger affect you?

3. True or false quiz

WORKSHEET 1: ANGER IS...

Introduce this worksheet (1a) – a true or false quiz designed to make children process the content of the first handout. Assist children in thinking about the questions and going back to what was read and discussed in the first handout.

Next, distribute the answer sheet (1b) to all participants, and let them check the answers as a group. This activity can be done in a fun way and you may offer rewards for right answers. Go over any questions which were answered incorrectly.

DISCUSSION

How did you find the questions? Were they hard or easy? What did you get wrong and why?

4. Anger management strategies

Introduce the concept that anger can be managed. Drawing from the content of the second worksheet and second handout, ask the group to discuss some strategies that may be useful in coping with anger (a whiteboard may be used to record these).

WORKSHEET 2: ANGER MANAGEMENT FOR KIDS

After the group has brainstormed ideas, give each child a worksheet to record their own strategies, and encourage them to commit to trying these whenever they feel angry. Distribute the second handout as a summary of ideas.

WORKSHEET 3: MINDFULNESS EXERCISE

Using this worksheet, children focus on the present and their five senses. Facilitate their ability to practise mindfulness activities and teach them to apply this strategy when they are angry, as being mindful will decrease angry feelings. Mindfulness is an active process that involves active attention, leading to awareness. It highlights the present, rather than the past or future. By default, mindfulness emphasizes acceptance and encourages children to see experiences as neutral rather than good or bad. The way to achieve mindfulness involves reflecting on external senses such as sights, sounds, smells, touches and tastes. Through mindfulness, children can learn to accept their emotions rather than fight them.

DISCUSSION

How do you feel about those strategies? Do you think they would work if you were angry? Why? Why not? How could you ask Mum, Dad or your carers to help you implement them?

ACTIVITY: MAKING FACES

Building on the body language and relaxation exercises in the previous session, ask the children to practise making 'angry', tense faces and to observe how it feels and looks. Then ask them to relax and observe how it feels and looks.

DISCUSSION

How did you feel about that activity? How did your face and body feel when you acted angrily? What about when you relaxed? Do you think that relaxing your face would help if you felt angry?

5. Ending activity: Making an 'Angry Crazy Box'

PURPOSE:

To teach children a healthy emotional release when angry. For children to understand that it is normal to get angry and that there are healthy ways to cope with anger.

RESOURCES:

- enough old muesli bar boxes or small cardboard containers for each child
- newspapers, magazines to cut
- paper, pens and crayons
- stickers
- large pasta shells
- sticky tape.

Prepare tables in advance, making sure that the resources are within easy reach of everyone. Discuss emotions with children and continue to describe what anger feels like. Children should be able to understand that anger is healthy and not something to be ashamed or afraid of. However, they should also understand that there are acceptable and unacceptable behaviours when someone is angry. This hands-on activity is an opportunity to encourage all children to remind the group what those acceptable behaviours are and to foster a commitment from all children to try their selected anger management strategies in view of repsonding to anger in an acceptable manner. Tell the children to cut pictures out of magazines, to write words or draw pictures of things which make them angry on pieces of paper and encourage them to express themselves creatively in decorating their boxes. You may discuss with children their anger towards the person/event they chose, and attempt to normalize it, using the strategies taught today. When the children have finished the process of decorating their 'Angry Crazy Boxes', they may fill those with items they have cut out and drawn, scrunched up newspaper and the pasta. The pasta should be as large as possible to provide a good crunching effect. Finally, they seal their box with sticky tape. The whole group then moves outside (or somewhere appropriate) to jump on the Angry Crazy Boxes, visualizing the letting go of anger and hurt when the box is destroyed.

6. Conclusion

Summarize the lesson and the worksheets with the participants, building on what they have expressed and shared and using the points listed in the Summary.

SESSION 7: ANGER MANAGEMENT
Handout 1
What Is Anger?

How do you feel when you get angry? Do you stay calm or do you feel like breaking things? Have you ever lost your temper?

Everyone gets angry – adults and children alike. Anger is not a bad thing; it can actually be a very good thing. It can help us defend ourselves, and when kids are treated unfairly, anger can help them stand up for themselves. It's not about *not* getting angry. It's about *what to do* or *not to do* when you're angry.

What is anger?

Anger is an emotion just as important as happiness, sadness, fear and excitement. It should be felt and experienced, but in the 'right' way. If you don't release your anger, you will become like a volcano and explode. This could be pretty bad for those around you!

What makes you angry?

There are many things which could make you angry: some little things and some big things. For example, you may get angry when Mum or Dad tell you to clean your room, and when your friend refuses to play a game you like. You may also get angry when you see something wrong being done to yourself or someone else.

How can I tell when I'm angry?

Everybody is different, but some of the things people have described when getting angry are body changes such as getting sweaty, rapid breathing, clenching of the jaws or fists, and so on.

Some children describe other changes such as head and belly aches. Some children need to show their anger to everyone, and other children try to hide it for as long as they can. This can lead them to feeling sick and sad.

The clever thing to do is to find a healthy and balanced way to express our anger without hurting ourselves or others.

|

✓

How can I tell when someone else is angry?

Sometimes people around us are angry. We know this because their behaviours change. They may use a different tone of voice; they may walk away or slam the door. We need to remember that some people need to be left alone to calm down. Try to think about what is making the person angry and whether it is safe to stay near them. When they are calmer, and if this is safe, try to talk about the issue.

What should I do if I get angry?

If it's you who is getting angry, resist losing your calm. Do not take it out on your friends or family. If you're angry because Mum told you to empty the dishwasher, do not smash the plates or throw the knives. Not only may you get hurt but it will not solve the problem. You may be able to ask someone for help in calming yourself down. Talking about our feelings helps them go away. Remember the 'hand' exercise we did in the session on grief and loss and go to one of those trusted adults for help.

SESSION 7:   ANGER MANAGEMENT
Worksheet 1a
Anger Is...

For each statement below mark the
answer you think is correct.

		TRUE	FALSE	SOMETIMES
1.	Anger is bad – it's one of those things we'd be better off without.			
2.	You can be angry with someone you love.			
3.	If you get angry, you can't control your emotions.			
4.	Anger is the other person's fault.			
5.	I can do anything I like to someone when I'm angry so long as I don't hurt them physically.			
6.	It's better to hide your anger than express it.			
7.	When you're angry you can't think straight.			
8.	No one can help us with our own anger.			
9.	Girls don't get angry as often as boys.			
10.	Angry people are responsible for their behaviours.			
11.	When you're angry, you're in charge and have power.			
12.	Being angry all the time can make you sad and/or depressed.			
13.	When someone makes you mad, it's OK to hurt them.			

|

✓

Answers!

1. *Is anger bad?* Anger is not good or bad. It's an emotion and it's neutral. It's what we do with that emotion that is good or bad (e.g. being angry at your sister for using your DS is OK, but telling her she's a stupid fat cow is not OK).

2. *Can you be angry with someone you love?* Of course you can! The closer you are to someone, the more likely you are to get angry with them. That's OK, and good communication skills and respect can help solve the issues that are making you angry. (It's OK to be angry with a friend but talking about it might help change the situation.)

3. *Can you control your emotions when you get angry?* Well, yes and no. Our brain is not in control for the first 13 seconds of us being angry but *we are* in control after that time. So if Mum tells you that you can't get something you really want today, it's OK to show anger initially. But what we know is that after the first 13 seconds, our brains have the ability to control our anger. It's therefore not OK to allow ourselves to do things we would usually find unacceptable. Use the happy thoughts exercises and look for positives.

4. *Is anger the other person's fault?* No. Someone might push our buttons; someone might be unfair to us; but it's how we see that situation that makes us angry. We still have a choice to walk away, tell a teacher or parent or to do something that can calm us down. (We'll learn some of these strategies today.)

5. *Can I do anything I like to someone when I'm angry as long as I don't hit them?* NO! Sometimes words hurt more than actions. It is not acceptable to say horrible things to anyone just because you're angry. Scaring, offending and name calling are not appropriate ways to express anger and you will hurt your friends and family for a long time that way.

6. *Is it better to hide your anger than express it?* Storing your anger by hiding it does not solve the problem, but if you're going to express it in a bad way, that's not helpful either. The best solution is to process anger safely in a way that does not hurt others or yourself.

|

7. *Can you think straight when you're angry?* If you're using the automatic part of your brain – not thinking about things – then you're probably not thinking straight. If you learn to 'think' about things before reacting, you will think straight even when angry.

8. *Can someone help me with my anger?* YES! Someone like Mum or Dad, a family member, a teacher or a counsellor can help you by listening to you, helping you to see another perspective or by solving your problems. Always reach out to someone.

9. *Do girls get angry as often as boys?* Of course they can; it's like everything else – it depends on your personality, not your gender. However, society has made it 'normal' for boys to get angry and not girls. This is wrong. Both boys and girls can get angry and it's not acceptable for either of them to hurt others.

10. *Are angry people responsible for their behaviours?* ABSOLUTELY! We are all responsible for our behaviours when we get angry – no excuses allowed.

11. *Do I have power when I'm angry?* NO, who are we kidding? Anyone who allows anger to control them has *no* power. I mean, how can you be powerful when you have no control?

12. *Can being angry a lot make me depressed (sad)?* YES, the chemicals in our brain (called serotonins) are used up when we become angry and this, on top of the negative thinking that gets us angry in the first place, can make us feel down and sad. The solution? Happy thoughts and practice in relaxation!

13. *Is it OK to hurt someone when you're angry?* NO! It's not OK for anyone to hurt someone else because they're angry. It's not OK to punch them, pinch them or make them trip over and it's not OK to call them names, scare them or bully them because we're angry. If someone does this to you or behaves like this around you, you should talk to someone else about it (e.g. Mum, Dad, teacher, counsellor).

SESSION 7:   ANGER MANAGEMENT
Worksheet 2
Anger Management for Kids

Anger is a very real emotion and is sometimes difficult to handle. What could you do to express your anger safely and constructively (in a way that helps everyone)?

Make a list of things you can do to release your anger:

1. ....

2. ....

3. ....

4. ....

5. ....

6. ....

7. ....

8. ....

9. ....

10. ....

Every time you get angry, start with your first strategy on the list and work your way down until you feel better.

To help you remember, you might want to stick this list on your wall, your door, desk or fridge!

SESSION 7: ANGER MANAGEMENT
Handout 2
Anger Strategies

Here are some other things you can do when you start to feel angry:

- Have a drink of water.
- Count to 15.
- Get or give a hug.
- Do star jumps or other exercises.
- Make an 'Angry Crazy Box'.
- Play on your computer or games console.
- Sing your favourite song.
- Listen to relaxing music.
- Practise the relaxation exercises we learned.
- Think bright and bubbly thoughts.
- Take a bike ride, go skateboarding, play basketball outside.
- Talk to someone.
- Write in your journal.
- Walk away.

You will continue to get angry in the future and that is normal. Focus on releasing healthy and constructive anger. You're the boss of your anger!

✓

SESSION 7: ANGER MANAGEMENT
Worksheet 3
Mindfulness Exercise

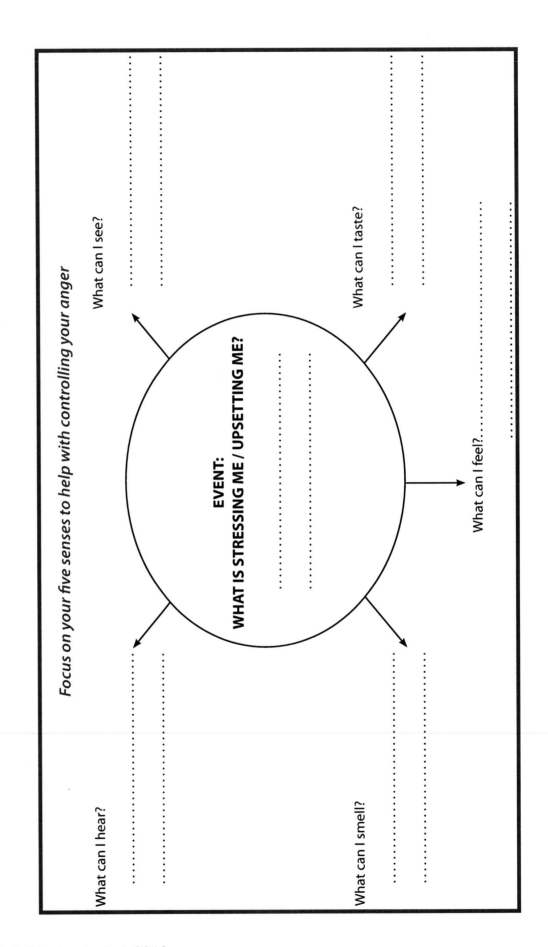

Focus on your five senses to help with controlling your anger

What can I see?

EVENT:
WHAT IS STRESSING ME / UPSETTING ME?

What can I taste?

What can I feel?

What can I hear?

What can I smell?

SUMMARY

'Anger management for kids!'

- Anger is a normal emotion and we need to learn to process it – not hide it or explode at other people.

- We are responsible for our behaviour, even when we get angry.

- Relaxing your body can help in controlling your anger. Practise those relaxation exercises on your own.

- We came up with a list of things you could do when you get angry. Practise the things you wrote on the list.

- Make an 'Angry Crazy Box' when you're angry and use it to calm yourself down.

WEEKLY TIP FOR PARENTS

- Ask your child about the 'Anger is…' true or false quiz we did and discuss the answers with them.

- If possible, ask your child to show you the anger management exercises we did and maybe practise them together.

- Make an 'Angry, Crazy Box' with them of something that is making you (or both you and them) angry or upset and discuss the process of letting go of the anger together.

Session | 8

Healthy Relationships Part 1

Holly and Hally are sisters who didn't get on before…
But now they have become symbols of great, healthy
relationships. They teach children about how to
recognize or address good relationships.

|

SESSION 8: HEALTHY RELATIONSHIPS MODULE 1
Peer Pressure

1. Greeting the participants and introduction to the session

Relationships are important in everyone's life. As children get older, they develop stronger and wider relationships with others, which will include parents, siblings, friends and girlfriends/boyfriends. Low self-confidence and poor communication skills, as well as genuine social anxiety, will prevent children from forming healthy bonds or recognizing peer pressure and bullying – things which can affect children on a social, physical and emotional level.

This module will attempt to teach participants about healthy relationships and the effects of peer pressure. Welcome the children back for their eighth session. Dedicate a few minutes to debrief on the application of the anger management skills taught in the last module and to facilitate socialization amongst the group. You may invite participants to share examples of how they combatted their anger and what they chose to do to release it safely and constructively – what worked and what didn't? Now introduce the topic of healthy relationships and verify the children's understanding of peer pressure. Allow everyone to take a turn.

Now present Holly and Hally. Explain that the girls are pretty close friends now, although it wasn't always the case. As sisters, they fought all the time, at school and at home! The meteor got them too, but since that moment, they have learned to have healthy relationships and now get along perfectly. Remind the group that they could all benefit from learning about relationships. After all, relationships are everywhere. Provide Holly and Hally's comic strip to the group at this point.

2. What are good friends and not-so-good friends?

WORKSHEETS 1–4: HEALTHY RELATIONSHIPS; FAMILY RELATIONSHIPS; RELATIONSHIPS WITH FRIENDS; DATING RELATIONSHIPS

Present the children with the series of worksheets on healthy relationships, which include family, friends and dating. The dating section should only be presented to groups of children who are of dating age or upon the request of the parents. The group may choose to take turns at reading the worksheets. Discuss content in each context as opportunities occur.

WORKSHEET 5: HEALTHY RELATIONSHIPS QUIZ

Next, present the children with the quiz and encourage them to try to find the answer. You may choose to offer small prizes such as mini chocolate bars or stickers for winners.

DISCUSSION

How do you feel about your relationships? Do you think they are healthy? Unhealthy? Why? What do you think is important in a relationship?

---

3. Who can I trust?

Introduce the next section of the session, which involves recognizing who children *can* and *can't* trust.

WORKSHEET 6: TRUST – TO GIVE OR NOT TO GIVE?

Distribute the sixth worksheet to the children, who may read as a group. Invite them to think about one relationship they are involved in (it may be a good or a bad one) and how it makes them feel. Discuss whether those are good feelings or bad feelings.

WORKSHEET 7: GINGERBREAD MAN

Using the seventh worksheet and the relationship they have chosen in the previous exercise, children may colour in the gingerbread man using the appropriate emotions/colours. Following this exercise, the group may discuss whether those colours imply that the person should be trusted or not.

Remind participants that they should use the Magical Formula when talking to their friends or bullies as well as their assertiveness skills. Encourage them to use the ABC Model and bright and bubbly thoughts when talking to friends.

DISCUSSION

Do you know who you can trust? How do you feel about what you've learned in regard to who you can trust and how to work it out? Do the colours/emotions you chose for the gingerbread man worksheet match how you feel about the person?

---

4. Ending Activity: Role-Playing

PURPOSE:

To assist the children in recognizing trustworthy and untrustworthy behaviours and to encourage participants to practise assertiveness skills in relationship contexts.

RESOURCES:

- printed character tags

- printed scenarios.

Children should be sitting in a group, either on the floor in a circle or at a table, in a manner that encourages team spirit. Retrieve and cut out the role-plays and tags in the Scenarios and the Character Tags Sheets. You may choose to attach the character tags to the scenarios in advance of the session. Each child is given a part to play, either as a main character or in a 'supporting' role (e.g. a 'mother' or a 'brother'). If time permits, allow every child the opportunity to play a main role.

Give children ten minutes to discuss their role-plays with fellow participants and decide how they will act the 'right way' using assertive, confident and healthy methods in the assigned story. After this time, each group demonstrates the role-play in front of the whole group. You should ensure that all children encourage each other and provide positive feedbacks.

5. Conclusion

Summarize the lesson and the worksheets with the participants, building on what they have expressed and shared and using the points listed in the Summary.

SESSION 8: HEALTHY RELATIONSHIPS PART 1
Worksheet 1
Healthy Relationships

Healthy relationships are great and make you feel good about yourself. They can also make you feel safe and valued.

What makes a relationship healthy?

Communication and sharing: Two friends should be able to listen to each other and take turns at sharing things. True friends will not repeat each other's confidences nor make fun of them. Lying and dishonesty do not belong in healthy relationships.

Respect and trust: Fighting with your friend will happen and this is normal. However, in a healthy relationship, friends will stay calm and talk about how they feel. They will try to figure any problems out. Respect is important, and friends should feel comfortable together.

How do I know that I have a healthy relationship with someone?

- Do you feel good about yourself when this friend is around? Or do you feel scared, angry and anxious?

  ....

- Are you the one working hard in the relationship? Is it always you giving your time or do you and your friend give it an equal amount of give-and-take? Do you feel that your friend is giving you the same attention as you give?

  ....

- Do you feel safe? Can you trust your friend with your secrets? Do you actually want to spend time with this friend?

  ....

Learning to keep relationships healthy NOW is important! It will help you have healthy relationships as adults. If you think you are in a bad relationship now, tell an adult or someone you trust!

SESSION 8: HEALTHY RELATIONSHIPS PART 1
Worksheet 2
Family Relationships

I fight with my mum and dad all the time because they always want me to clean up my room. My brother always uses my bike and I hate it! It's like they're all on the same side!

Our family can upset us at times. We may not always understand what they are saying or why they're saying it. However, they love you and you love them, and by using good communication skills, you can all get along better. It is very normal for children to be overwhelmed by their parents and siblings or to imagine that life would be better without them. Your relationship with your parents may be difficult. As children are growing into teenagers, they have more responsibilities and more freedom. Sometimes children feel that they are ready to make decisions but parents may set limits on this. It's important to remember that parents may do this to protect their children from others and various dangers.

There are some things you can do to make life easier for everyone.

Here are some examples:

- Go to your room to cool down.

- Talk to your parents about the issues.

- Respect your family.

- Take turns at using the phone, TV, toys and video games.

- Choose your battles – not everything is worth fighting for!

- Negotiate the rules as a family, if possible.

- Commit to the rules.

- Spend time with your family (it will make you feel closer!)

Add your own ideas:

- ....

- ....

- ....

- ....

- ....

SESSION 8: HEALTHY RELATIONSHIPS PART 1
Worksheet 3
Relationships with Friends

We used to be best friends but recently we have been fighting about which games to play or where to hang out. It's like things are different now!

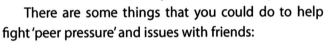

Our relationships with friends change over time and become complicated at times. Some friends will move on and you will also make new and different friends. Sometimes 'peer pressure' happens. This is when your friends ask you to do, or you feel that you should do, things you wouldn't normally (e.g. smoking, drinking or being mean to others). You may be worried about what others will think and this may lead you to do particular things. It is important to learn to be assertive and say 'no' to these things.

There are some things that you could do to help fight 'peer pressure' and issues with friends:

- Say 'no' to your friends from time to time. You have the right to say 'no' to your friends whenever you want to. True friends will not judge you or leave you because of this.

- Don't be afraid of healthy debates. Arguing is normal in *all* friendships.

- Don't hang onto friendships which are 'over'. Friendships change over time – some will end and new ones will happen. This is normal.

- Value friends and treat them right! Friendships are important.

Add your own ideas:

- ....
- ....
- ....
- ....
- ....
- ....
- ....

SESSION 8: HEALTHY RELATIONSHIPS PART 1
Worksheet 4
Dating Relationships

Dating can be awkward at first. You may have met someone who you'd like to get to know more but do not know what you're supposed to do now.

You should not feel pressured to date. Young people need to be ready to enter dating relationships. They need to be honest with their parents about their relationships and what they are doing. Some of your friends may start dating before you and you may feel 'pressured' to do the same. Not everyone is ready at the same time and you should not rush into a dating relationship.

A healthy dating relationship is similar to a healthy friendship. It should be honest, trustworthy and respectful. What you give to the other person should be something with which you're comfortable. You should be able to discuss those things with your parents to ensure you remain safe and that you are legally permitted to engage in those activities. You may just want to hold hands or kiss. You should not feel pressured to give any more than what you are willing to.

You should be able to talk to someone you trust about this special relationship and get support on how to handle it. Remember to balance all your relationships equally: friends, family and dates.

Some things may be helpful in achieving this:

- Get to know a person first before dating them.

- Go out with a group of friends to a public place on your first few dates.

- Plan fun and safe activities (e.g. movies, beach, theme park).

- Have clear boundaries with the other person.

- Have clear boundaries with your parents.

- Always tell an adult about where you're going and who with.

- Enjoy those relationships, have fun and take it step-by-step.

Add your own ideas:

- ....

- ....

- ....

- ....

- ....

- ....

SESSION 8: HEALTHY RELATIONSHIPS PART 1
Worksheet 5
Healthy Relationships Quiz

Tick the answer you think is correct:

1. Some very important parts of any relationship are:

   a) Communication and sharing, and respect and trust.

   b) Communication and giving in, and respect and tricking.

   c) Silence and TV, and trust and tantrums.

2. You know you're in a healthy relationship when:

   a) You feel safe when you shut your belongings away or hide them.

   b) You feel safe with the person, you give and take turns at things equally, and you feel good about yourself.

   c) You ask for money and the person always gives in.

3. Some of the things you can do when your sister/brother is annoying you are:

   a) Talk to your parents about what is bothering you.

   b) Leave the room until you're calmer.

   c) Take turns at choosing games and TV programmes.

   d) All of the above.

4. Peer pressure is bad and happens when:

   a) You choose to do something you wouldn't normally do because you're afraid your friend will laugh (e.g. smoking, drinking, bullying others).

   b) You stop doing things you would normally do because you're afraid your friends will stop being your friends (e.g. homework, being nice to your parents and siblings, dressing a particular way).

   c) You feel pressure from being stuck in an elevator for two hours with your friend.

   d) Both a) and b).

5. Some of the things you could do to help with peer pressure are:

   a) Talk to a grown-up about it (e.g. parents, teachers, friends' parents).

   b) Tell the person pressuring you how you feel, and be true to yourself.

   c) Tell yourself that you know what the right thing to do is, even when friends are laughing at you.

   d) Change friends and find better friends.

   e) Give in to the bully.

   f) Answers a), b), c) and d).

6. By being . . . . , your relationship with your parents will improve:

   a) Stubborn and disrespectful.

   b) Calm, polite and willing to communicate.

   c) Asleep all day and messy.

SESSION 8:   HEALTHY RELATIONSHIPS PART 1
Worksheet 6
Trust – to Give or Not to Give?

You don't need to trust someone right away. Also you can take your trust back if someone breaks your trust in them. So here are some steps to follow to work this out:

1. What do you know about them? (What do others say? What does your gut say?)

2. So what does that tell you? Do you think they are worthy of your trust? YES or NO?

3. Do their actions match what you think you know about them? YES or NO?

4. You have the right to change your mind.

5. Repeat these steps as often as you need to.

Example:

- Someone tells you that you should trust them but you just saw them steal something from someone's bag. What does your gut tell you?

- Someone tells you that you should trust them and all their friends love that person. What do you think now?

SESSION 8: HEALTHY RELATIONSHIPS PART 1
Worksheet 7
Gingerbread Man
Feelings are something you feel in your body

Illustrate the gingerbread man with the colours representing your feelings. For example, if you feel nervousness in your belly, colour the gingerbread man's belly orange.

Sad – Blue

Fear – Black

Guilt – Brown

Anger – Red

Jealous – Green

Nervous – Orange

Happy – Yellow

Excited – Purple

Emotionless – No colour

Thinking about the relationship you have with somebody else, how do you feel inside your body? Do you feel happy, do you feel sad or do you feel angry? What do those feelings tell you about your relationship with that person? Could you do something to improve it? Should the relationship end?

✓

SESSION 8: HEALTHY RELATIONSHIPS PART 1
Scenarios

✂ ....

Your friend makes fun of you because you've just politely said 'goodbye' to your mum. He tells you you're a baby.

✂ ....

You walk past a group of girls/boys in the toilet at the movies and they make fun of what you're wearing.

✂ ....

Your group of friends all decide to shave their heads. You don't really know what you'd like to do. They tell you that you have to do it to be in their club.

✂ ....

Your brother tells your mum that he saw you at the canteen being stupid. Your mother does not seem angry.

✂ ....

You're invited to a party. The person who invited you really gives you creepy vibes. You really don't want to go. All your other friends are going.

✂ ....

✂ ....

At the dinner table, your brother/sister keeps interrupting you as you're trying to tell your family things about your day. You are getting really frustrated.

✂ ....

Your teacher says something (e.g. 'You're wasting my time' or 'You are late') and you are not sure whether it is meant to be a personal attack or whether you're over-reacting. Her tone is hard to read.

✂ ....

All your friends have the latest phone, laptops and other gadgets. Your parents tell you that they can't afford one or that they don't believe it's good at your age. You go to school and everyone asks you what kind of phone you have.

✂ ....

Your best friend comes to school crying. She is really upset because her parents had a huge fight last night. She tells you that she wants to run away. You're feeling sad and overwhelmed too.

✂ ....

You're just about to hop in the shower when your brother pushes you out of the way, gets in the bathroom and prepares to have a shower himself. You suspect he knew you were going to use the bathroom.

✂ ....

SESSION 8: HEALTHY RELATIONSHIPS PART 1
Character Tags

You may choose to copy and attach all character roles to each case-scenario to assist on the day of role-plays. Detach each role and distribute to the children in the team acting the role-play.

Friend	*Parents*
You	*Dad*
Teacher	*Student in class*

|

✓

Mum	Person inviting you
Sister	Friend
Bully	Brother

|

SUMMARY

'Healthy Relationships!'

- There are healthy and non-healthy relationships. It's important to be able to recognize both types.

- Remember to read the worksheets on relationships with an adult and discuss them.

- Let an adult know if you believe you are currently in a bad relationship with a friend or anyone else, or being bullied.

- Remember the Magical Model to communicate assertively and the ABC Model to think bright and bubbly thoughts (positive thinking)…USE, USE and USE these strategies!

WEEKLY TIP FOR PARENTS

- If possible, ask your child to show you the worksheets and exercises and practise with them.

- Encourage them to act confidently with others, especially those who want to hurt them verbally.

- Practise scenarios if need be.

Session | 9

Healthy Relationships Part 2

|

SESSION 9: HEALTHY RELATIONSHIPS MODULE 2

1. Greeting the participants and introduction to the session

The topic of healthy relationships is an ongoing one especially as the children develop into young people. Peer pressure, bullying and social influences are recognized as real, unavoidable and often traumatic experiences. The skills taught in both the previous and current module should be described as skills which will improve over time. It should be emphasized that those skills are vital in healthy relationships.

In welcoming the children back for their ninth session, you may take a few minutes to debrief on the application of the skills taught in the last week and facilitate the socialization of the group. Remind the children that the programme is reaching its end and that there is only one session remaining. Some of the participants, particularly those with attachment issues, anxiety or unresolved grief and loss, may need some forewarning and adjustment time. Invite the children to share examples of how they have observed their relationships and to describe potential peer pressure examples.

2. Can I do anything if I'm bullied?

HANDOUT 1: FACTS ABOUT BULLYING

Introduce the topic of bullying, perhaps by asking the children about their understanding of bullying and whether they, or someone they know, have ever experienced bullying. Explain that bullying is something that can happen to any of us. It happens when another person or a group of persons do and say things to us to hurt us, scare us or take advantage of us, and it makes children feel really vulnerable. Next, present the first handout to the participants. Attention should be paid to any children who exhibit trauma symptoms or have been victims of bullying.

DISCUSSION

Have you ever been bullied? What happened? How do you know it was bullying? How did you feel? Did you tell anyone? Why? Why not?

WORKSHEET 1: THINGS I CAN DO IF I'M BULLIED

Distribute the first worksheet (on strategies against bullying) and read the strategies as a group. This should be done in a safe and nurturing way as some of the participants may have suffered bullying and may associate it with fear, shame or anxiety. Ensure that you normalize those feelings and encourage children to discuss their experiences and thoughts.

DISCUSSION

How do you feel about those strategies? Would they work for you? Yes? No? Why? What other strategies can you think of?

3. Our 'Wise Warrior Protection'

After allowing a good debriefing on bullying and ensuring that all children get the opportunity to share their experiences, introduce the concept of 'Wise Warrior Protection'. The wise warriors in the old countries used to talk about their invisible and noble protective coats. The story should be shared in an uplifting and exciting narrative way.

Explain that the wise warriors who used to live in the mountains in the old countries were always very strong. They valued nature and other people, and always resisted revenge attacks. Tell the children that in today's session they are going to learn about the values the warriors shared and how they used their magical protection to protect themselves against other people's words and thoughts.

DISCUSSION

What qualities can you see in yourself? In other people? Can you imagine yourself as a strong and wise warrior? How would this protect you from other people's words and thoughts?

WORKSHEET 2: QUALITIES OF A WISE WARRIOR

Distribute the second worksheet. In this exercise children are encouraged to discuss their values and strengths. Point out how they may all have different traits circled and how these influence who we are and can protect us. The children should be able to read the words correctly – you will need to explain the values to younger children. Participants should be encouraged to reflect on the meaning behind each word and find examples of how it may or may not apply to them.

WORKSHEET 3: THE WISE WARRIOR SHIELD

Explain how to use the magic protection against ill words. This worksheet should be used in conjunction with a narrative and illustrative story. Ensure that participants understand the concept of protecting ourselves from reacting to negativity and provocation, and engage in the imaginary aspect of the exercise.

'There were once strong warriors living up tall mountains. They had promised their ancestors that they would teach their children about their noble spiritual values. The warriors were robust, yet they were meek. Every time someone tried to provoke them, they reminded each other of their covenant and responded in a gentle way.'

4. Ending activity: Making a Shield Representing 'Wise Warrior Protection'

PURPOSE:

To assist the children in identifying their values and to create an imaginary protection against bullying, as well as teaching them not to attack back if possible.

RESOURCES:

- coloured cardboard in the shape of shields (one for each child)
- glitter glue
- feathers
- leaves
- ribbon
- old magazines
- pencils
- any other collage material.

Prepare tables in advance, spreading the resources evenly. Be as creative as you can, with the provision of bright, varied and multiple types of resources, which may include, seeds, feathers, leaves, glitter, coloured paper, magazines, foil, and so on.

Pre-draw the shield shapes on large strong cardboard sheets (you may also choose to precut these). Ask the children to decorate a shield with symbols highlighting their strengths, wisdom and values, which will serve as a protection against negative influences. During this process, continue to reinforce the principles discussed during the lesson, such as preventing and addressing bullying, as well as reinforcing the children's values and strengths. Praise the children for their efforts and final products. Children should be encouraged to hang up their shield in their room (or other place where they will see it often) to remind them of their invisible protection.

5. Conclusion

Summarize the lesson and the worksheets with the participants, building on what they have expressed and shared and using the points listed in the Summary.

SESSION 9: HEALTHY RELATIONSHIPS PART 2
Handout 1
Facts About Bullying

What is bullying?

Bullying is when one person does or says things to another person to hurt or intimidate them. They may be using name calling, spreading rumours about them, hitting them, scaring them or forcing them to do things they don't want to do.

Why do some people bully?

Some kids are bullies because it makes them feel strong, gives them attention and makes them look 'tough and mean'. Some bullies have been bullied themselves or do it because they feel bad about themselves in general.

Why is bullying bad?

Kids who are bullied feel sad, scared and do not always learn to stand up for themselves. It can affect them for a very long time. Some kids actually get sick or refuse to go out because of it.

Should I do something if someone else is being bullied?

Yes, you should try to stop it or go to an adult who can help. Let the person being bullied know that they can go and tell someone.

Can I make it stop if it happens to me?

YES! There are strategies designed to make bullies stop and we will learn some today.

◻ SESSION 9:   HEALTHY RELATIONSHIPS PART 2
Worksheet 1
Things I Can Do if I'm Bullied

- Stop and count to five.
- Talk with the bully if you think you can and it is safe to do so.
- Talk in your head, saying things such as 'I'm OK' (don't react).
- Stand up for yourself with calm words.
- Go to a safe place.
- Talk to someone about what is happening (parent, teacher, principal, adult friend).
- Ignore the bully, walk away or change the subject.
- Say something that shows you're in control (e.g. 'I've got better things to do than listen to this').
- Look confident even if you're not. (Practise in private or with a trusted friend or an adult.)

Add your own:

- ....
- ....
- ....
- ....

✓

HEALTHY RELATIONSHIPS PART 2
Worksheet 2
Qualities of a Wise Warrior

Circle the qualities that you can recognize in yourself:

Heroism   Dynamism   Excellent at what you do

Willing to have a go   Determination   Ambition

Sets goals   Never gives up   Fearlessness

Responsible   Overcomes fears

Generosity   Shares   Gives   Self-sacrificing

Spiritual awareness   Noble qualities   Integrity

Honest   True to themselves   Makes the right choices

Respectfulness   Treat others with consideration

Polite   Friendly   Resourcefulness

Jumps at all opportunities   Survivor

Finds solutions to problems

SESSION 9: HEALTHY RELATIONSHIPS PART 2
Worksheet 3
The 'Wise Warrior' Shield

When someone attacks you or sends you unfriendly vibes, it's easy to attack back in self-defence. Most of the time the person wants you to attack back to get power over you.

RESIST ATTACKING BACK!

Wrap your imaginary Wise Warrior shield around you to protect yourself so that the other person's actions don't affect you. Imagine them sliding off you or dropping to the ground. Stay calm and watch the other person knowing that you are calm and safe.

Who do you know that wears a Wise Warrior shield? Who never attacks back? Who always seems at peace? . . . .

. . . .

Remember:

Your Wise Warrior shield is always with you.

- It strengthens you.

- It never hits back.

- You can use it wherever you want.

- Hurting others damages the power of the Wise Warrior shield.

- Don't attack back. Remain peaceful.

- Be wise but not crazy. If you're physically attacked 'get out' and always call an adult.

SUMMARY

'Healthy relationships and bullying!'

- There are healthy and non-healthy relationships. It's important to be able to recognize each type.

- Let an adult know if you believe you are currently in a bad relationship with a friend or anyone else, or are being bullied.

- We discussed what to do in case of bullying – practise this!

- Focus on your personal Wise Warrior protection (your personal power and protection against people who try to attack you). It is powerful, strong and nothing can hurt you if you keep it on. The only exception is if someone tries to hurt you physically – in this case, you should get away and call an adult for help at all times.

WEEKLY TIP FOR PARENTS

- If possible, ask your child to show you the worksheets and exercises and practise with them.

- Encourage your child to act confidently with others, especially those who want to hurt them verbally.

- Allow them to put their Wise Warrior shield up in their room to remind them of what it represents.

Session | 10

Healthy Minds in Healthy Bodies

We all know the old saying: 'A healthy mind is a healthy body'. This is exactly what Beau is about.

|

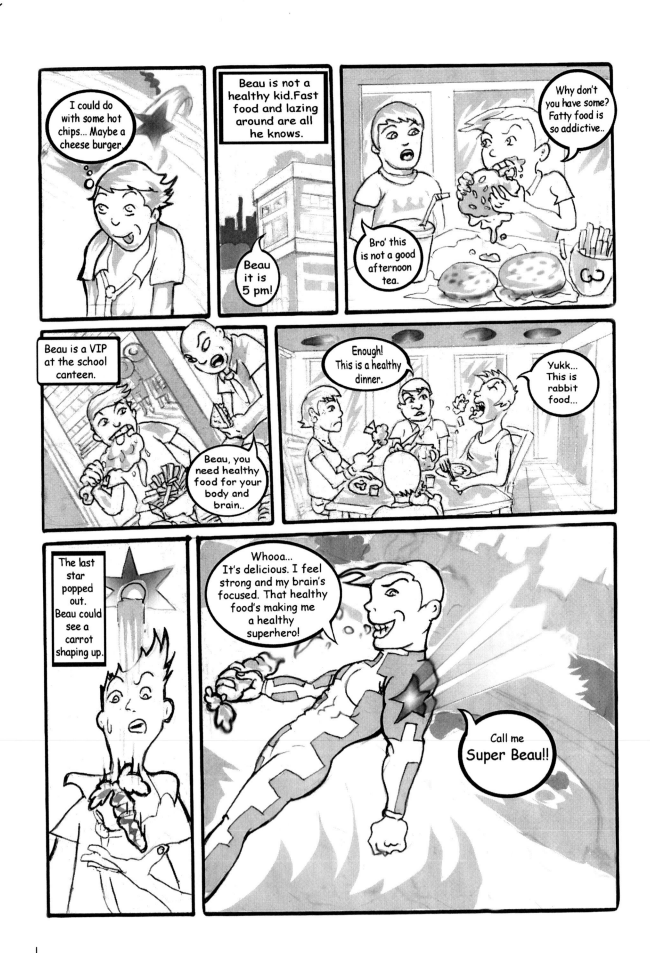

SESSION 10: HEALTHY MINDS IN HEALTHY BODIES MODULE

1. Greeting the participants and introduction to the session

This module is the last one of the programme. As an important session, it holds a double purpose: to teach the children about healthy bodies and to provide the opportunity for the children to debrief on the programme, evaluate it and facilitate closure. Some of the children, particularly those with attachment issues, may struggle with terminating the course. It may have been a positive source of emotional debriefing and friendship-forming, and you should be mindful of the dynamics and individual children's adjustment.

Welcome the children back and gently remind them that it is the last session of the programme. You may break the ice by inviting the children to share examples of how they combatted bullying and whether it worked or didn't work. When the participants have all had the opportunity to share their experiences, you may introduce the topic of healthy bodies and healthy minds and assess the children's understanding of health and grooming.

Explain to the children that Beau is the last character for the programme. Beau was a junk food lover. He would eat unhealthy food and watch TV all day. After he was hit by the meteor, he started craving healthy food and lived a balanced lifestyle. Encourage the group also to strive for a balanced lifestyle and provide them with Beau's comic strip. Continue by explaining that once the Super Kids came together, they made a commitment to teach those ten skills to children around the world. Provide the group with the last four pages of the comic book. Remind children to put together the whole comic book from the beginning and remember the Super Kids' lessons.

2. Healthy bodies

WORKSHEET 1: WHAT MAKES A HEALTHY BODY?

Distribute the first worksheet – the participants may take turns reading it aloud. Assist the children in defining what healthy eating, healthy exercise and healthy grooming are. Additionally, you may help children find examples.

DISCUSSION

What does a 'healthy body' mean to you? Do you think you have one? Who around you do you feel has one? Could you improve on any of those areas (eating, exercising, grooming)? How?

WORKSHEET 2: HEALTHY BODIES AND HEALTHY MINDS

Distribute this worksheet and discuss ways to improve the three areas of healthy eating, healthy exercise and personal grooming. The children should fill in the blanks individually. The group shares their answers and everyone should be allowed to express their thoughts on the topic. Ensure that everyone feels safe to discuss their bodies and encourage children to be mindful of others' feelings about it.

Now introduce the concept of healthy eating by explaining to participants that different food items give us different degrees of energy, fat, sugars and proteins. Continue by explaining that eating more calories than we use will result in putting on weight, eating fewer calories than we use will result in losing weight, and eating about the same will result in staying the same weight.

WORKSHEET 3: MATCHING FOOD WITH THE RIGHT PHYSICAL ACTIVITY

Using the third worksheet, the children draw a line from an item of food to a physical exercise, trying to match the amount of work they would have to do to stay about the same weight. You may add or alter the options to anything suitable. The value of the activity lies not in the answers themselves, but in the discussion around the possibilities.

The answers are as follows:

1. A glass of chocolate milk ———— A five-minute bike ride.

2. An apple and some sultanas ———— Writing in your journal.

3. A burger from a fast-food restaurant ———— Jogging for about 30 minutes.

4. A ham and lettuce roll ———— Walking from the car park to your class.

5. Fifteen chocolate cookies ———— Jumping very high 200 times on a trampoline.

DISCUSSION

Are you surprised about the answers? Did you ever think about food and exercise this way? How could you become more balanced when it comes to healthy eating?

3. Ending Activity: 'Going Out for Dinner'

PURPOSE:

For children to understand that eating should be moderated, varied and include healthy food; to realize that eating junk food should come with extra activity to avoid putting unhealthy weight on.

Children should be told that under-eating is just as unhealthy as over-eating and that both will lead to feeling bad about themselves and potentially make them ill.

RESOURCES:

- the list of available 'dinners' on the Dinner Activity Sheet, printed in multiple copies and cut out (you may design new ones to suit the group and taste of participants at your discretion).

The children may sit on the floor in a circle or may be seated at a table. Stack the dinner tags (main courses and desserts) in piles in front of the participants. No further details should be shared with children, so as not to influence them in their food choices. Ask the participants to help themselves to the food tags they would like to eat for dinner (e.g. lasagne and potato chips or a brownie with ice cream). Once the children have chosen their item(s), discuss with them that in real life the food we choose equals an amount of exercise that we have to do to remain healthy.

Finally, the children find out that each item of food they chose came attached with an exercise as follows:

- Potato chips = 30 crunch-ups.
- Lasagne = 30 crunch-ups + a fast walk.
- Crumpet with honey = 15 star jumps.
- Brownie with ice cream = jumping on the spot for five minutes + 20 crunch-ups.
- Fruit salad = a brisk walk around the room/courtyard.

This activity involves children having to do the exercises. The activity should be fun and non-punitive – the children should not feel threatened or on display (especially children who may be overweight or have issues with body image).

Close the programme by summarizing the teachings over the last ten modules and inviting the children to continue working on their strengths and weaknesses. Using motivational interviewing techniques, the facilitator should allow children to feel motivated, uplifted and proud of their growth and successes. It is recommended that you hand evaluation forms (found in the appendix) to all children, who may fill these in anonymously if they wish and return them to you. Finally, introduce the last activity to close the programme. This may take the form of a breaking-up party if appropriate. Evaluation forms can be found as an appendix at the back of the programme.

Additionally, you may ask the parents/carers/teachers to fill in an evaluation form as per your discretion and invite parents/carers to come in for:

1. parental evaluation

2. remittance of final summaries and attendance certificates.

4. Conclusion

Summarize the lesson and the worksheets with the participants, building on what they have expressed and shared and using the points listed in the Summary.

5. Closing activity of programme: 'The Person I Was; the Person I Am'

PURPOSE:

For children to identify their areas of growth and to feel motivated and hopeful about change, and to assist children in realizing and verbalizing what they have achieved in the programme.

RESOURCES:

- photocopies of the 'Person I Was/Am Now/Am Becoming' Closing Activity Sheet on coloured paper or card

- water paints, pencils, felt pens, charcoal, chalk and other drawing material

- magazines.

Prepare tables in advance so that resources are accessible equally to all participants. Explain the concept of growth and tell the children that they should reflect on who they were *before* they started the programme and represent this by writing, drawing or pasting pictures from magazines. They will then reflect on who they are *now*, or who they are becoming, and represent this as well. Encourage children to describe the differences observed and share them with the group. This activity should be organized in a positive and safe environment, ensuring that all children leave with a feeling of accomplishment. Finally you should encourage participants to continue practising the skills they have learned and praise them for the changes they have embraced.

SESSION 10: HEALTHY MINDS IN HEALTHY BODIES
Worksheet 1
What Makes a Healthy Body?

We all should strive to have healthy bodies. Eating healthy food, exercising regularly and grooming ourselves are things that will make us feel good and fit. Let's talk about what those things mean for us.

1. Healthy eating

We need to eat a variety of food. Some foods are 'everyday' food and others are 'sometimes' food. We need to pay attention to what we're eating and how often. It is important to eat lots of fresh fruits and vegetables and to love our bodies. It's not about our shape but about being healthy!

2. Healthy exercise

We need to exercise for at least 30 minutes per day, and at least three times a week according to the experts! It may be that we can walk to school instead of catching a bus or we may be able to jump on a trampoline after school. It is important to exercise every day but within limits. Too much can be a problem too!

3. Personal grooming

Cleaning our teeth, brushing our hair and regularly changing our underwear and socks might sound funny but did you know these things are really important to personal grooming? Some examples may be wearing a special outfit or special earrings. These are of course only suggestions. There are no rights or wrongs. It is about what makes you feel nice.

What does having a healthy body mean to ME?

....

....

....

....

....

SESSION 10: HEALTHY MINDS IN HEALTHY BODIES
Worksheet 2
Healthy Bodies and Healthy Minds

Personal grooming is important. Some examples of things you may enjoy thinking about may be your hair, nails or clothes. Again, it is about what makes you feel good about yourself.

What personal grooming means to me: ....

....

....

Healthy eating is important. Not only will I feel better, be more energetic and think more clearly when I eat healthy and balanced food, but I will also stay in the healthy weight range.

What healthly eating means to me: ....

....

Exercise is important. Not only will it help me to be healthier overall, and to maintain a healthy weight, but it will also release endorphins in my brain which will make me happy and stress free.

What exercise means to me: ....

....

SESSION 10: HEALTHY MINDS IN HEALTHY BODIES
Worksheet 3
Matching Food with the Right Physical Activity

Draw a line from an item of food on the left to an activity on the right that you would need to do in order to remain healthy and balanced.

Jogging for about 30 minutes

A five-minute bike ride

Jumping very high 200 times on a trampoline

Writing in your journal

Walking from the car park to your class

1. A glass of chocolate milk

2. An apple and some sultanas

3. A burger from a fast-food restaurant

4. A ham and lettuce roll

5. Fifteen chocolate cookies

SESSION 10:   HEALTHY MINDS IN HEALTHY BODIES
Dinner Activity Sheet
List of Dinners

A serving of potato chips with gravy

A crumpet with honey

A serving of lasagne

A brownie with ice cream

A fruit salad

SESSION 10: HEALTHY MINDS IN HEALTHY BODIES
Closing Activity Sheet

'The Person I Am Now or Am Becoming'

'The Person I Was'

SUMMARY

'Healthy Mindsets for Super Kids – *closing of the programme!*'

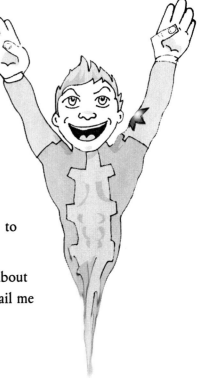

- We discussed healthy lifestyle choices. Remember, your body is an extension of your mind and you need to feel good about both.

- Remember to take pride in your appearance. If you make yourself look good, you will feel better about yourself!

- Remember to wear your imaginary protection when others try to hurt you or things bother you. Imagine the hurt sliding off your invisible cloak.

- Put your summaries together and read them from time to time.

- Remember always to find someone you trust to talk to about anything that is bothering you. You are welcome to email me or ring me any time.

CLOSING NOTE TO PARENTS

Dear Parents,

Today marks the last session of the *Healthy Mindsets for Super Kids* programme for your child. It has been a privilege to get to know them.

In some cases, your child will have learned skills they will be able to use. For others, there may still be a way to go to achieve the resilience you're after. Remember that when we work with children, we look at the whole family and not just the child, because in the family's dynamic we often find the reasons a child has developed one way or another (e.g. divorce or relationship status, discipline and parenting methods, communication skills, your own anger management, your own thinking patterns, your own grief and loss, amongst other things). This is *not* a bad thing, but a *normal occurrence* in every family. I would encourage all of you to look at your child in a family context and apply some of the teachings they have learned to the whole family.

Appendices

The following photocopiable sheets have been provided for your information and benefit. Facilitators may use the following templates when advertising and promoting their course. Appropriate spaces have been left for facilitators to add their own details. For more information please contact info@stephanieazri.com or visit www.stephanieazri.com.

List of sheets:

- Programme flyer
- *Healthy Mindsets for Super Kids* application form
- Attendance sheet
- Attendance certificate for children
- Feedback form for children
- Feedback form for parents.

Healthy Mindsets for Super Kids

Healthy Mindsets for Super Kids is a resilience programme for children aged 7–14. The programme is at (location) . . . . on (dates) . . . . from (time) . . . .

The course is facilitated by (name) . . . . with qualifications and experience in . . . .

Some of the sessions will address:

- Positive self-image
- Communication skills
- Assertiveness training and social skills
- Positive thinking
- Grief and loss
- Healthy bodies in healthy minds
- Anger and frustration management
- Anxiety and stress management.

The cost is . . . . per child for the whole programme and covers costs. This particular programme is designed for children who have early symptoms or as a preventative intervention.

To enquire about having *Healthy Mindsets for Super Kids* run in your local school, contact your school principal with a copy of this brochure.

(Signature)

(Business details)

(Name)..

(Business Details)..

Application to join *Healthy Mindsets for Super Kids*

Name of children: .... Age: ....

School and year level: .... Tel:.......................................

Address: ....

Email or mobile number for notification: ....

Who referred you to the programme? ....

Reasons for wanting to join programme:

....

....

....

....

....

....

....

RELEVANT child and family history:

....

....

....

....

....

....

....

Signature:..

✓

Healthy Mindsets for Super Kids Attendance Sheet

NAME	Paid	Session 1	Session 2	Session 3	Session 4	Session 5	Session 6	Session 7	Session 8	Session 9	Session 10

Certificate of Attendance

Awarded to:

_____

For successfully completing the
Healthy Mindsets for Super Kids resilience programme.

Modules include:

- Self-Esteem
- Communication Skills
- Anger and Frustration Management
- Grief and Loss
- Positive Thinking
- Healthy Relationships
- Body Image

Keep up the good work!

. . . .
Facilitator   *Date*

|

✓

Healthy Mindsets for Super Kids

FEEDBACK FORM FOR CHILDREN

Dear Friend,

Thank you for participating in the *Healthy Mindsets for Super Kids* programme this term. I have enjoyed our time together and hope that you have learned a few skills you will use in the future.

I would really appreciate it if you could take five minutes to fill in this form for me. It will help me provide an even better programme for other children in the future. I'd love to hear how the programme helped you down the track.

NAME (optional): ....

What did you enjoy the most in *Healthy Mindsets for Super Kids*? (A particular activity, a particular session or something you learned?)

....
....
....
....
....
....

What did you enjoy the least in *Healthy Mindsets for Super Kids*? (A particular activity, a particular session or something that bored you?)

....
....
....
....
....
....

Overall, how would you score your experience in the programme (out of 10, 1 being bad and 10 being great)? Circle the number:

1	2	3	4	5	6	7	8	9	10

TERRIBLE   OK   AWESOME

How did you find the teacher (facilitator) and why?

....

....

....

....

....

Do you have any other comments?

....

....

....

....

....

....

....

Remember that you are welcome to contact me any time by phone or email to touch base or to talk about how you are getting on after the programme.

✓

Healthy Mindsets for Super Kids

FEEDBACK FORM FOR PARENTS

Dear Parents,

Thank you for enrolling your child in the *Healthy Mindsets for Super Kids* this term. I have enjoyed my time with them and hope that they have learned skills they will use in the future.

I would really appreciate it if you could take five minutes to fill in this form for me. It will help me provide a better programme for other children in the future. If appropriate, I'd love to hear how the programme helped your child down the track.

NAME (optional): ....

As a parent, what feedback did you get from your child regarding the programme?

....
....
....
....
....
....

Was there a particular session that was especially beneficial to your child?

....
....
....
....
....
....

Was there a particular session that was not well received by your child?

....
....
....
....
....
....

As a family and given your personal reasons for enrolling your child in the programme, have you noticed any changes in your child's symptoms or behaviour (less teary, less angry, happier)?

....

....

....

....

....

....

How would you rate the facilitator and why?

....

....

....

....

....

....

Overall how would you score your experience with the programme (out of 10, 1 being bad and 10 being great)? Circle the number:

| 1 | 2 | 3 | 4 | 5 | 6 | 7 | 8 | 9 | 10 |

UNSATISFIED   AVERAGE   HIGHLY SATISFIED

Do you have any other comments?:

....

....

....

....

....

....

Kindest regards,

....

|

References

Daniel, B. and Wassell, S. (2002) The School Years: Assessing and Promoting Resilience in Vulnerable Children. London: Jessica Kingsley Publishers.

Schoon, I. (2006) *Risk and Resilience: Adaptations in Changing Times.* Cambridge: Cambridge University Press.

Werner, T.T. (1993) 'Risk, resilience and recovery: perspectives from the Kauai Longitudinal Study.' *Development and Psychopathology 5,* 503–515.